Disney Theatrical Productions
under the direction of
Thomas Schumacher
presents

Disney
FROZEN
THE BROADWAY MUSICAL

Music and Lyrics by   *Book by*
KRISTEN ANDERSON-LOPEZ and ROBERT LOPEZ   **JENNIFER LEE**

Based on the Disney film written by JENNIFER LEE and directed by CHRIS BUCK and JENNIFER LEE

Starring

CAISSIE LEVY   PATTI MURIN

JELANI ALLADIN   GREG HILDRETH   JOHN RIDDLE

ROBERT CREIGHTON   KEVIN DEL AGUILA   TIMOTHY HUGHES   ANDREW PIROZZI

AUDREY BENNETT   MATTEA CONFORTI   BROOKLYN NELSON   AYLA SCHWARTZ

ALYSSA FOX   AISHA JACKSON   ADAM JEPSEN

ALICIA ALBRIGHT   TRACEE BEAZER   WENDI BERGAMINI   ASHLEY BLANCHET   JAMES BROWN III   CLAIRE CAMP
LAUREN NICOLE CHAPMAN   SPENCER CLARK   JEREMY DAVIS   KALI GRINDER   ASHLEY ELIZABETH HALE   ZACH HESS   DONALD JONES JR
NINA LAFARGA   ROSS LEKITES   AUSTIN LESCH   SYNTHIA LINK   TRAVIS PATTON   ADAM PERRY   OLIVIA PHILLIP
NOAH J. RICKETTS   ANN SANDERS   JACOB SMITH   NICHOLAS WARD

T0078622

Co-Producer **ANNE QUART**	*Technical Supervision* **AURORA PRODUCTIONS**	*Senior Production Supervisor* **CLIFFORD SCHWARTZ**

General Manager   *Associate Director*   *Associate Choreographers*
RANDY MEYER   **ADRIAN SARPLE**   **SARAH O'GLEBY**   **TELSEY + COMPANY**
                                                        CHARLIE WILLIAMS   **RACHEL HOFFMAN, CSA**

Orchestrations   *Executive Music Producer*   *Music Coordinators*   *Music Director*
DAVE METZGER   **CHRIS MONTAN**   **MICHAEL KELLER**   **BRIAN USIFER**
                                                        MICHAEL AARONS

Hair Design   *Makeup Design*   *Special Effects Design*   *Additional Dance Arranger*
DAVID BRIAN BROWN   **ANNE FORD-COATES**   **JEREMY CHERNICK**   **DAVID CHASE**

Sound Design   *Video Design*   *Puppet Design*
PETER HYLENSKI   **FINN ROSS**   **MICHAEL CURRY**

Scenic and Costume Design   *Lighting Design*
CHRISTOPHER ORAM   **NATASHA KATZ**

Music Supervision and Arrangements by
STEPHEN OREMUS

Choreographed by
ROB ASHFORD

Directed by
MICHAEL GRANDAGE

ISBN 978-1-5400-3126-6

Cover Artwork © Disney
Production photos by Deen van Meer
Disney Characters and Artwork © Disney

DISTRIBUTED BY

HAL•LEONARD®

Visit Hal Leonard Online at
www.halleonard.com

Contact Us:
Hal Leonard
7777 West Bluemound Road
Milwaukee, WI 53213
Email: info@halleonard.com

In Europe contact:
Hal Leonard Europe Limited
Distribution Centre, Newmarket Road
Bury St Edmunds, Suffolk, IP33 3YB
Email: info@halleonardeurope.com

In Australia contact:
Hal Leonard Australia Pty. Ltd.
4 Lentara Court
Cheltenham, Victoria, 3192 Australia
Email: info@halleonard.com.au

Mattea Conforti, Ayla Schwartz

Patti Murin

Jelani Alladin, Andrew Pirozzi

Jelani Alladin, Patti Murin

Caissie Levy

Patti Murin, John Riddle

A LITTLE BIT OF YOU

Music and Lyrics by KRISTEN ANDERSON-LOPEZ
and ROBERT LOPEZ

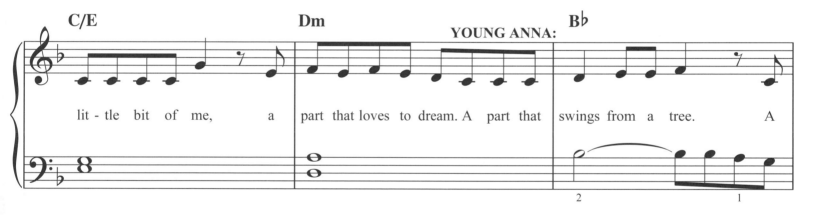

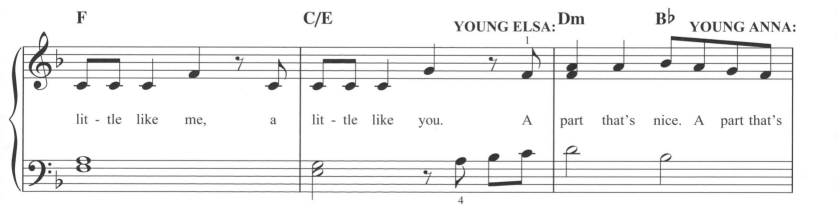

naugh-ty too.   A loy-al friend who is there no mat-ter what, with a

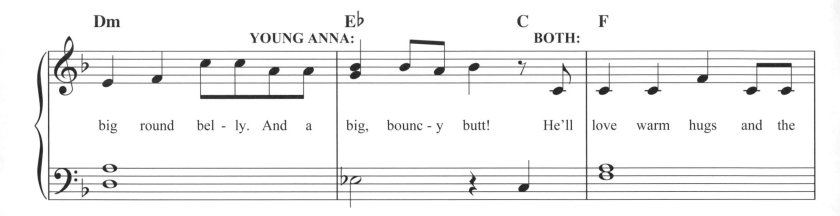

big round bel - ly. And a big, bounc-y butt! He'll love warm hugs and the

bright sun - light. And he'll real - ly love the sum - mer. But he'll

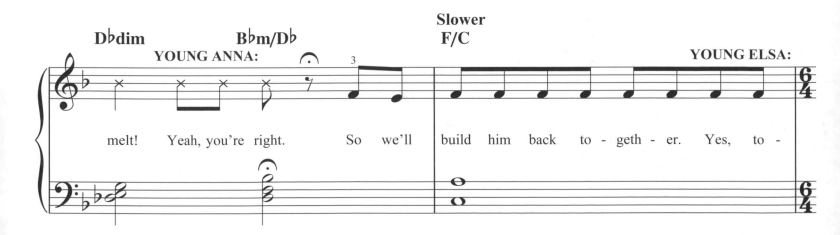

melt! Yeah, you're right. So we'll build him back to-geth-er. Yes, to -

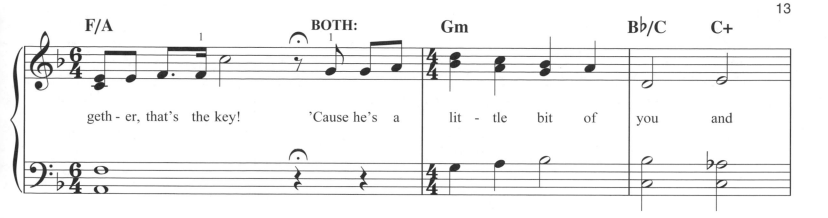

geth - er, that's the key! 'Cause he's a lit - tle bit of you and

YOUNG ELSA: *Okay, time for bed.*
YOUNG ANNA: *NO. Time for more magic please and thank you.*
YOUNG ELSA: *Anna, you know I'm not supposed to even be doing this.*

me.

YOUNG ANNA: *But your magic is the most beautiful wonderful, perfectful thing in the whole wide world.*
YOUNG ELSA: *Do you really think so?*
YOUNG ANNA: *Yes! So, do it, please, before I burst from inside to outside.*
YOUNG ELSA: *Okay, Okay. Don't burst.*

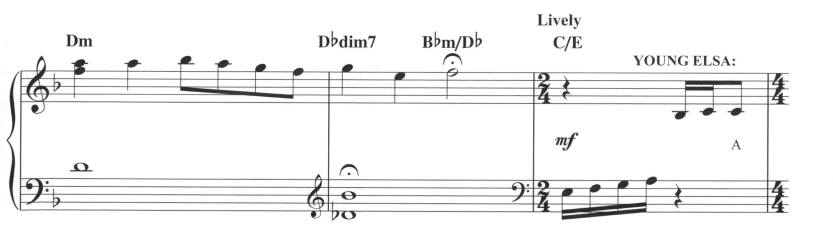

14

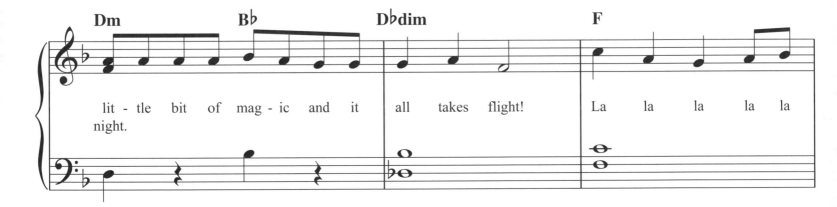

15

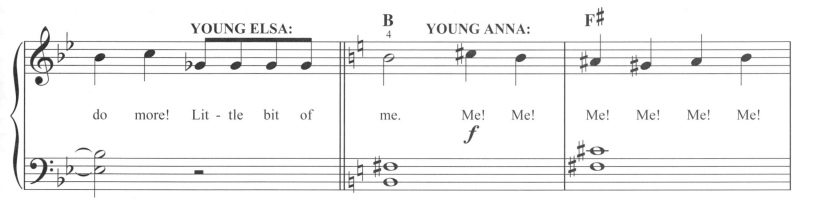

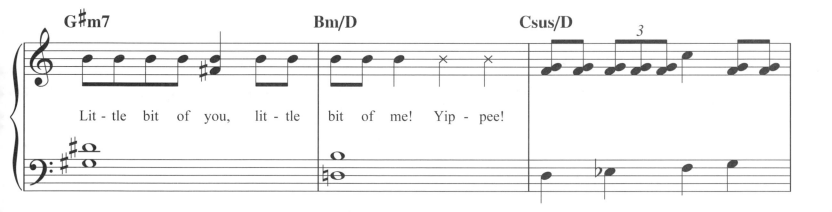

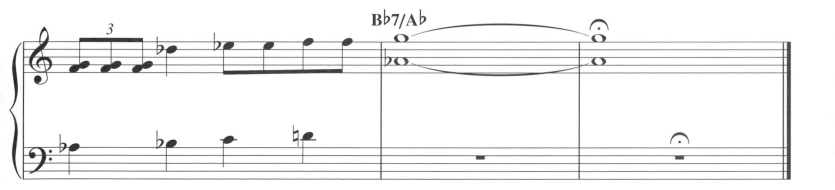

DO YOU WANT TO BUILD A SNOWMAN?

(Broadway Version)

Music and Lyrics by KRISTEN ANDERSON-LOPEZ
and ROBERT LOPEZ

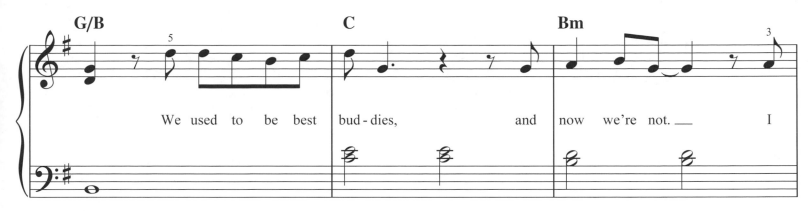

We used to be best bud - dies, and now we're not. ___ I

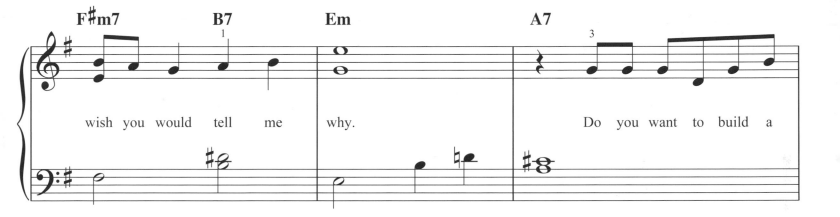

wish you would tell me why. Do you want to build a

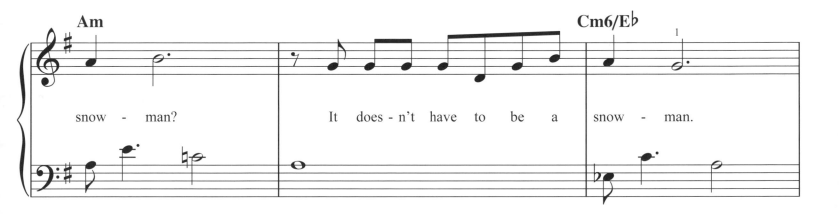

snow - man? It does - n't have to be a snow - man.

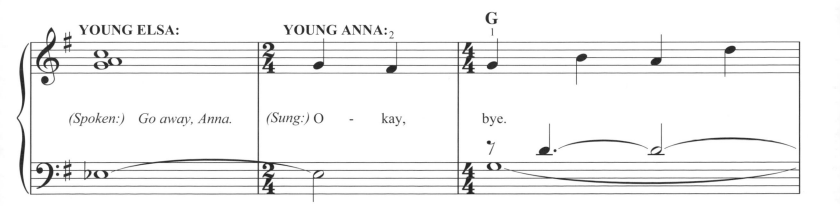

YOUNG ELSA: (Spoken:) Go away, Anna. **YOUNG ANNA:** (Sung:) O - kay, bye.

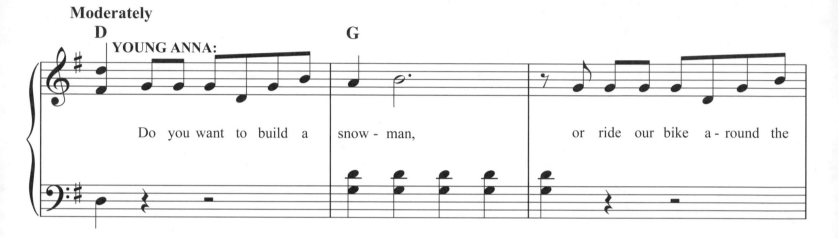

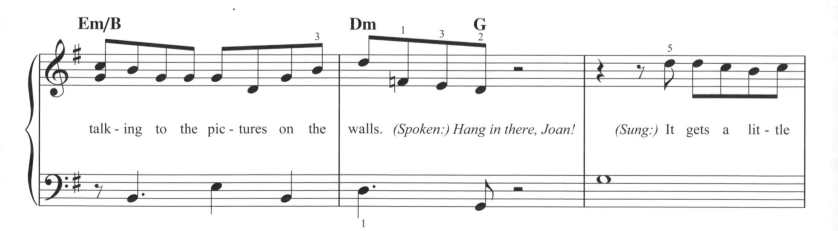

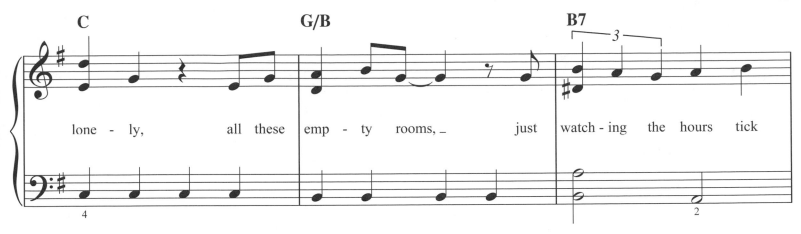

lone - ly,　　　all these emp - ty rooms, _ just watch - ing the hours tick

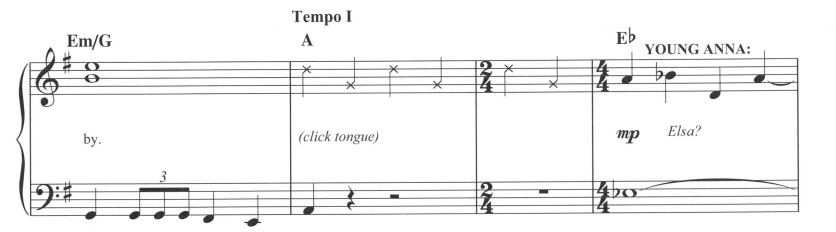

Tempo I

by.　　　*(click tongue)*　　　*mp* *Elsa?*

YOUNG ANNA:

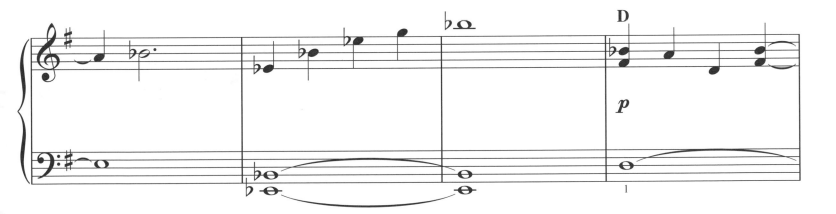

Elsa?

Slower, freely

G/D

(Sung:) Please, I know you're in there. I'm just won-d'ring how you've

mp

D/F♯

C/E

been. Do you may-be want to take a walk, or sit and

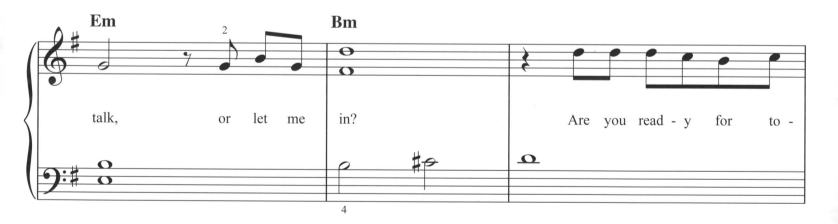

Em

Bm

talk, or let me in? Are you read-y for to-

C

D/F♯   G

B7sus/F♯   B7/D♯

mor-row? It's your big day! Is there an-y-thing I can

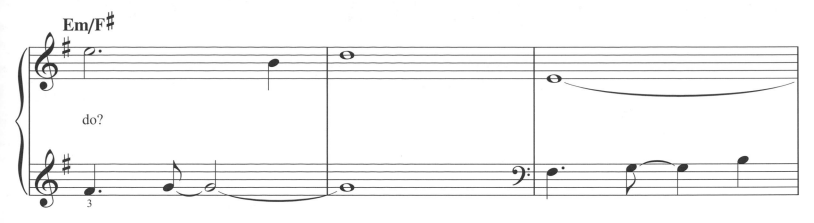

do?

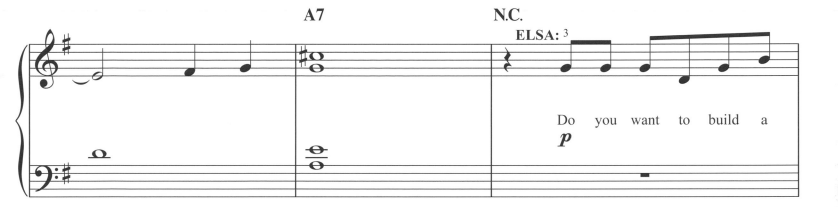

Do you want to build a

snow - man?

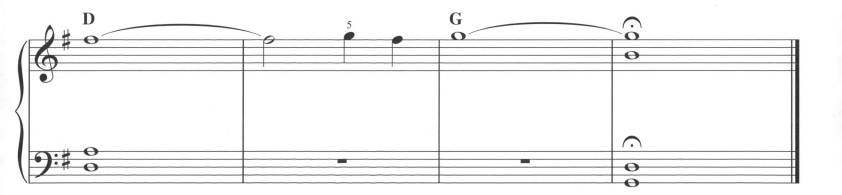

FOR THE FIRST TIME IN FOREVER
(Broadway Version)

Music and Lyrics by KRISTEN ANDERSON-LOPEZ
and ROBERT LOPEZ

With excitement

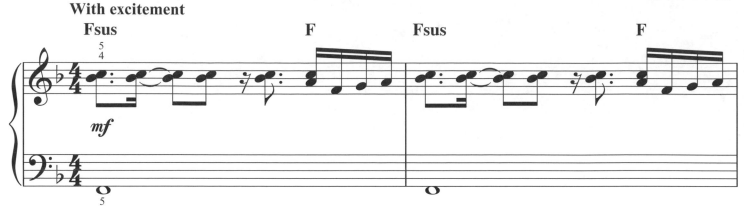

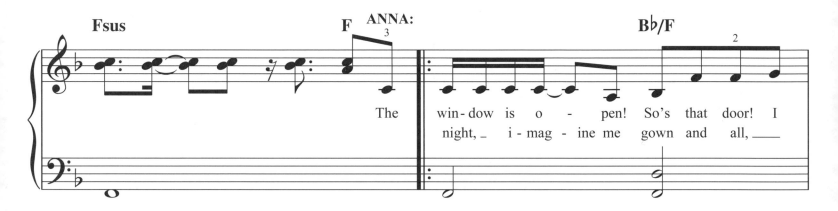

The win-dow is o-pen! So's that door! I
night, __ i-mag-ine me gown and all, ____

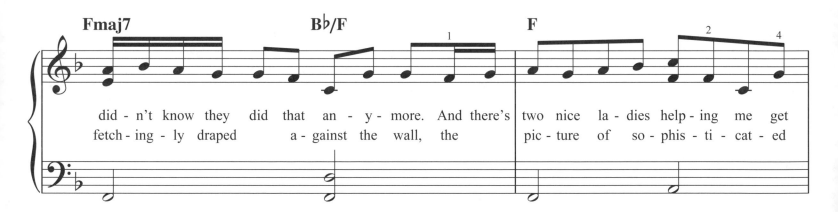

did-n't know they did that an-y-more. And there's two nice la-dies help-ing me get
fetch-ing-ly draped a-gainst the wall, the pic-ture of so-phis-ti-cat-ed

dressed! *Thanks!* For years I've roamed __ these emp-ty halls.
grace. I sud-den-ly see __ him stand-ing there, a

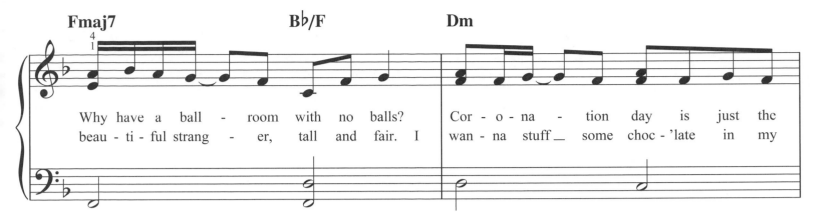

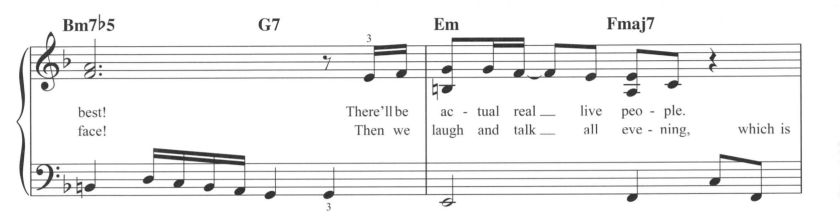

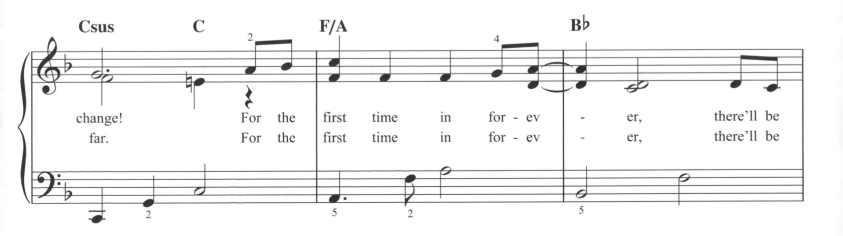

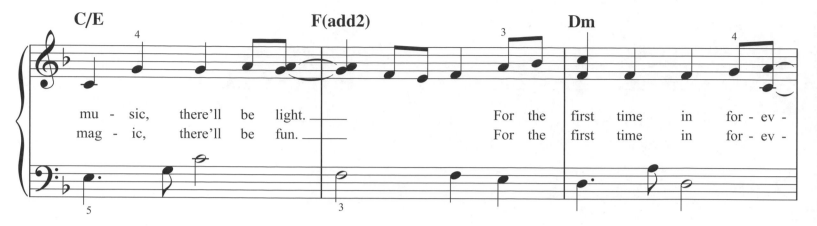

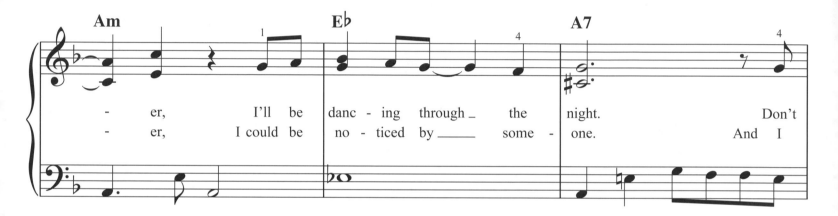

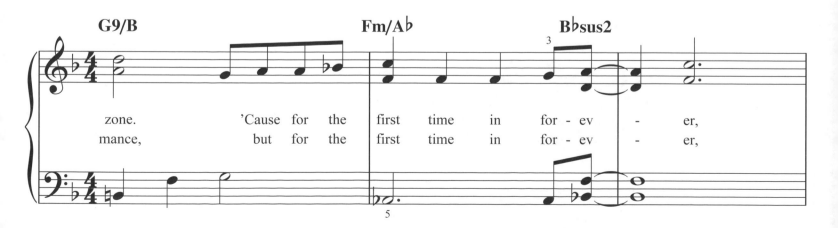

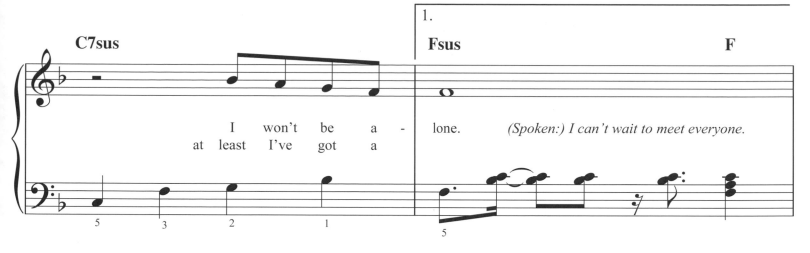

C7sus

1.

Fsus

F

I won't be a - lone. *(Spoken:) I can't wait to meet everyone.*
at least I've got a

Fsus　　　　　**F**　**Fsus**　　　　　**F**

(gasp) What if I meet...　　*THE ONE?*　　*(Sung:) To -*

2.

F　　　　　　　　　　　　　　**D**

chance.

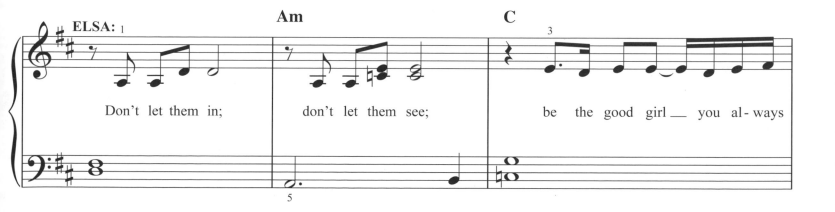

ELSA:　　　　**Am**　　　　　　**C**

Don't let them in;　don't let them see;　be the good girl ___ you al - ways

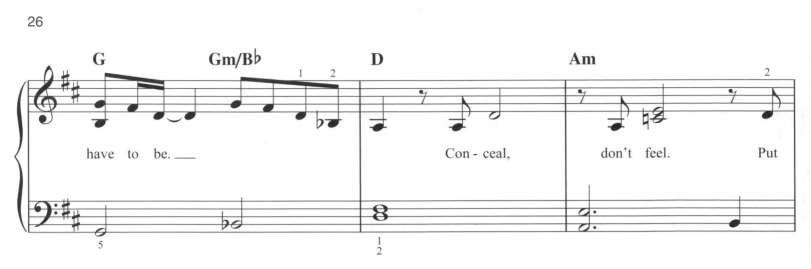

have to be. ___   Con - ceal,   don't feel.   Put

on a show,   make one wrong move, and ev - 'ry - one will

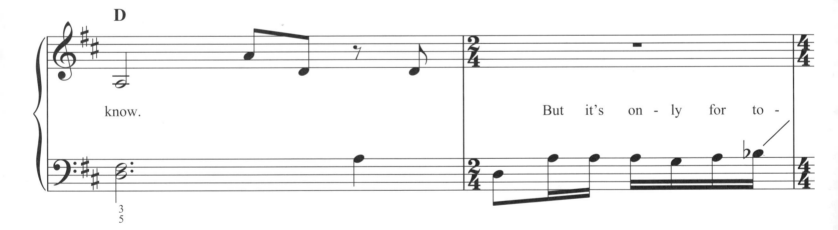

know.   But it's on - ly for to -

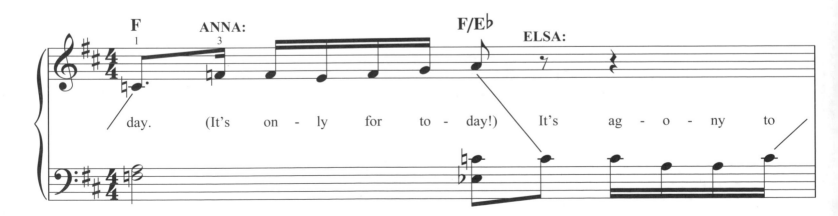

day. (It's on - ly for to - day!) It's ag - o - ny to

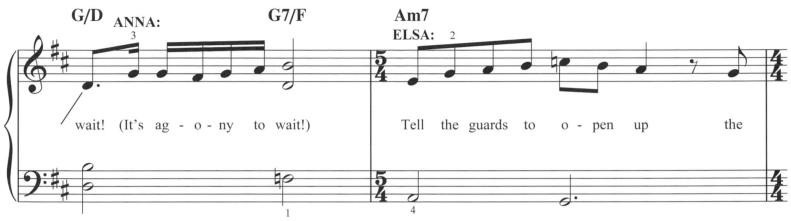

G/D ANNA: **G7/F**   **Am7** ELSA:

wait! (It's ag - o - ny to wait!)   Tell the guards to o - pen up the

F   ANNA:

gate!   The   gate! _____

G/B   **C(add2)**

___ For the first time in for - ev - er, I'm get - ting

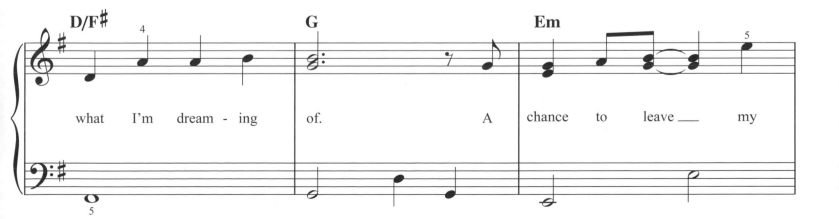

D/F♯   **G**   **Em**

what I'm dream - ing of.   A chance to leave ___ my

28

lone - ly world, a chance to find ___ true love. For the

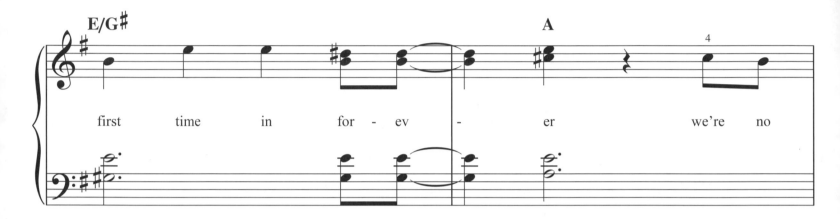

first time in for - ev - er we're no

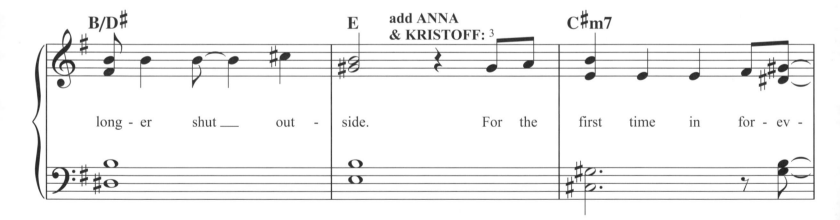

long - er shut ___ out - side. For the first time in for - ev -

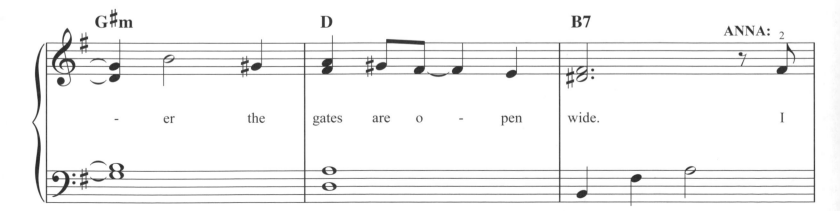

- er the gates are o - pen wide. I

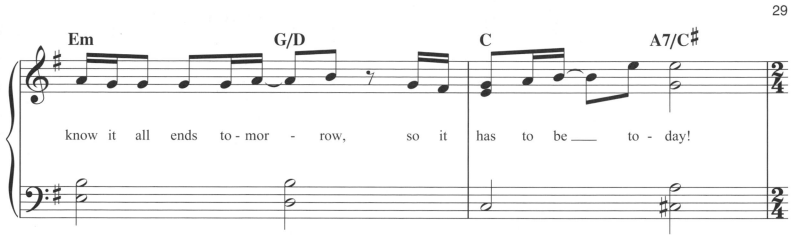

know it all ends to - mor - row, so it has to be ____ to - day!

'Cause for the first time in for - ev - er, for the

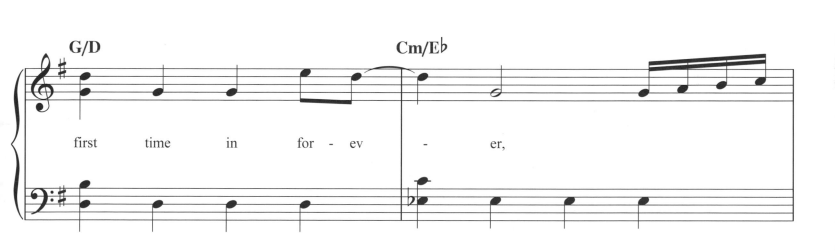

first time in for - ev - er,

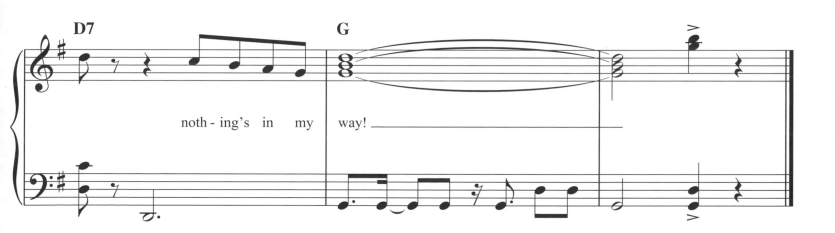

noth - ing's in my way! ____

HANS OF THE SOUTHERN ISLES

Music and Lyrics by KRISTEN ANDERSON-LOPEZ
and ROBERT LOPEZ

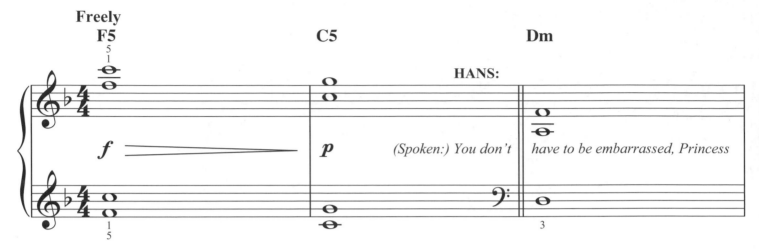

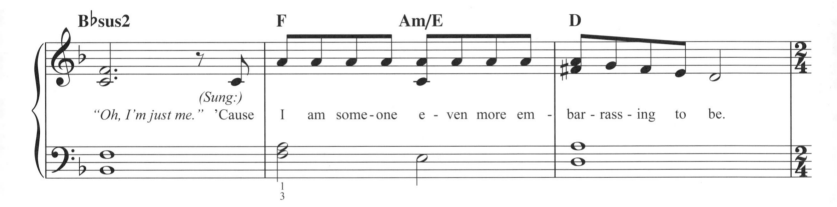

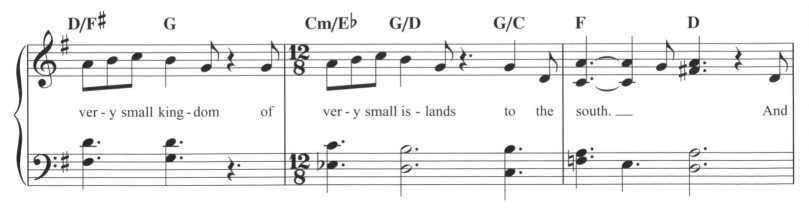

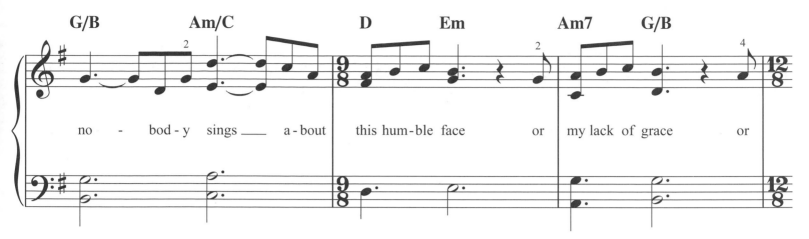

no-bod-y sings ____ a-bout this hum-ble face or my lack of grace or

quotes ____ what comes out ____ of my mouth. *Thank goodness.* I've

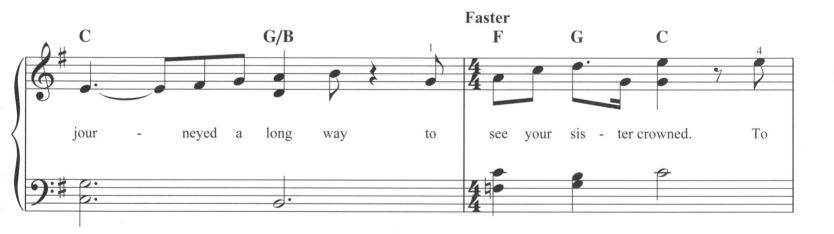

jour - neyed a long way to see your sis - ter crowned. To

hon-or and to back you, yet here I go and smack you to the ground. *poco rit.*

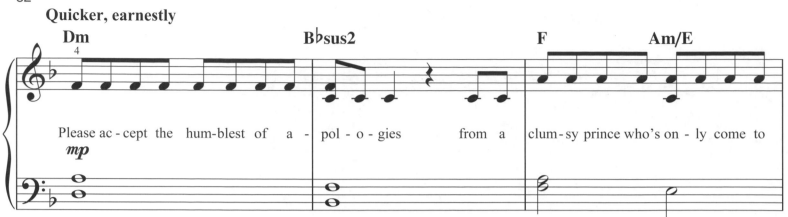

Quicker, earnestly

Please ac - cept the hum-blest of a - pol - o - gies from a clum-sy prince who's on - ly come to

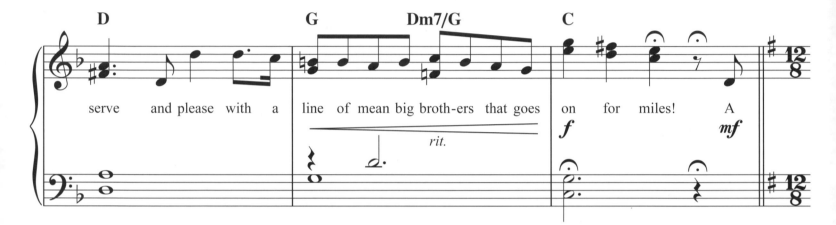

serve and please with a line of mean big broth-ers that goes on for miles! A

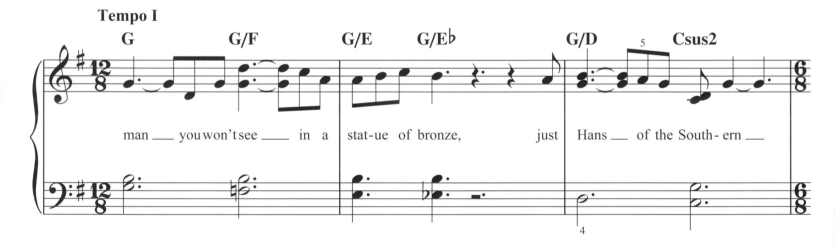

Tempo I

man __ you won't see __ in a stat-ue of bronze, just Hans __ of the South-ern __

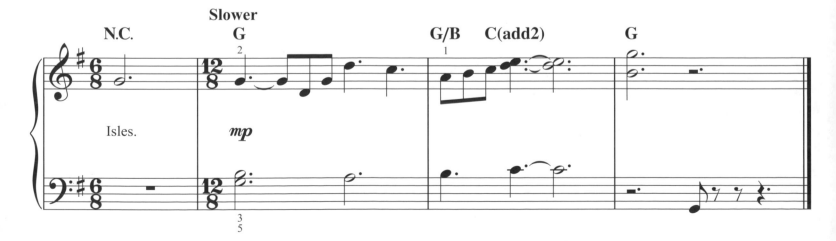

Slower

Isles.

DANGEROUS TO DREAM

Music and Lyrics by KRISTEN ANDERSON-LOPEZ
and ROBERT LOPEZ

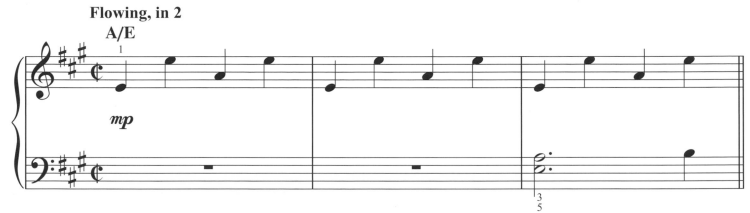

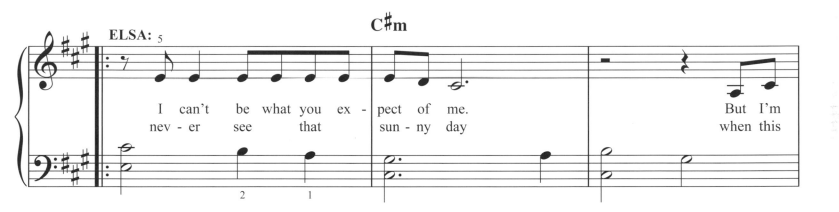

I can't be what you ex-pect of me.
nev-er see that sun-ny day
But I'm
when this

try-ing ev-'ry day ___ with all I do just and
trial is fi-n'lly through ___ and it could just be

do not say. Here, on the edge of the a-
me and you. I can't dwell on what we've

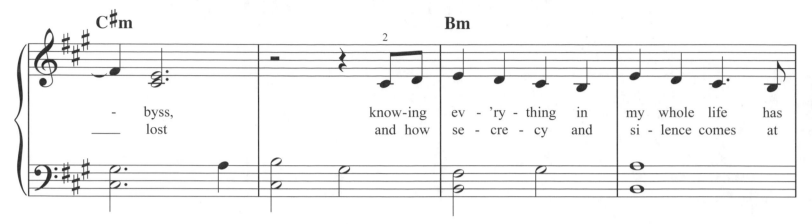

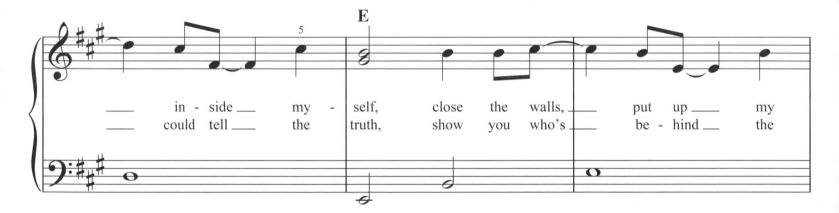

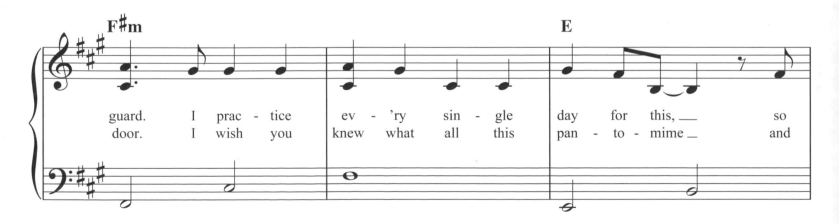

why is it ___ so hard?
pag - eant - ry ___ was for.

I have

'Cause I can't
have to be ___ so

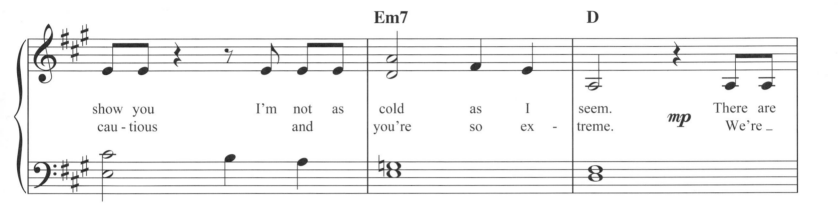

show you
cau - tious

I'm not as
and

cold
you're

as
so

I
ex -

seem.
treme.

There are
We're ___

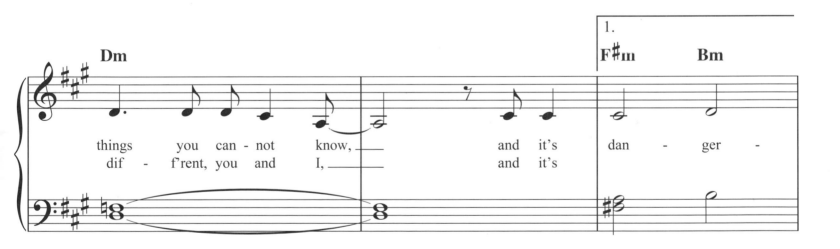

things
dif - f'rent,

you can - not
you and

know, ___
I, ___

and it's
and it's

dan - ger -

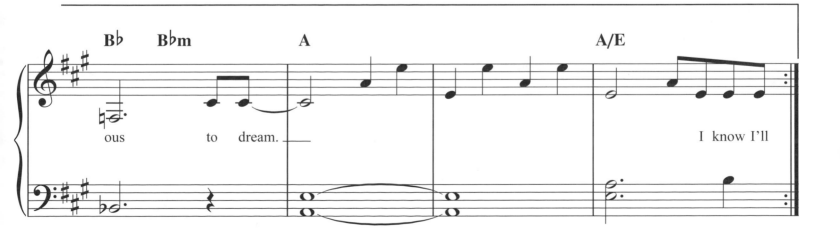

ous

to dream. ___

I know I'll

36

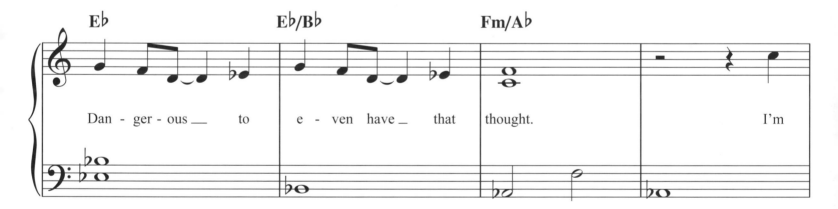

37

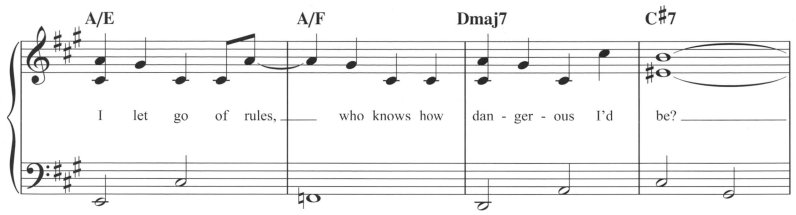

I let go of rules, _____ who knows how dan-ger-ous I'd be? _____

BISHOP: _____ *Your majesty,* | *the gloves.*

ELSA: Why right now would I make this mis-take?

How could I let my con-cen-tra-tion break?

(Spoken:) Conceal...don't feel...conceal...don't feel...

38

BISHOP:

(Spoken:)
Sem hon heldr inum helgum eignum ok krynd i pessum helga stao ek te fram fyrir yor... Queen Elsa of Arendelle.

rit.

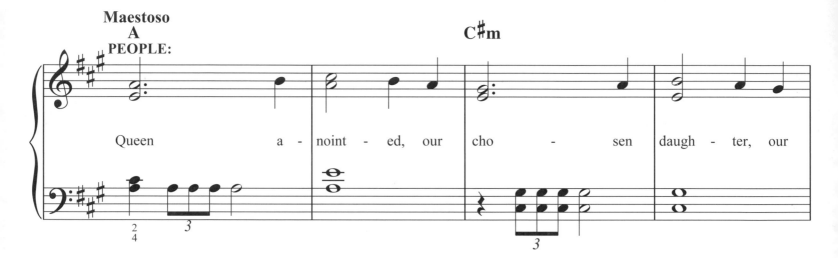

Maestoso
A
PEOPLE:

C#m

Queen   a - noint - ed, our   cho - sen   daugh - ter, our

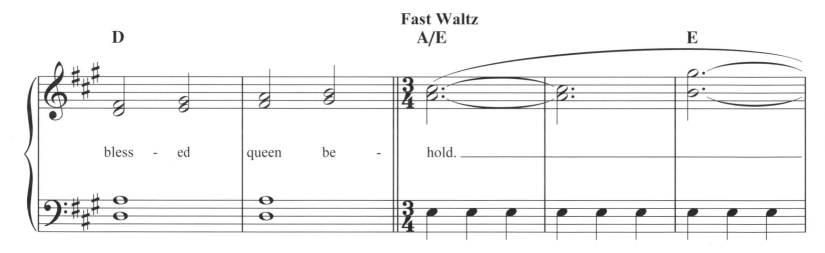

Fast Waltz
D   **A/E**   **E**

bless - ed   queen   be -   hold.

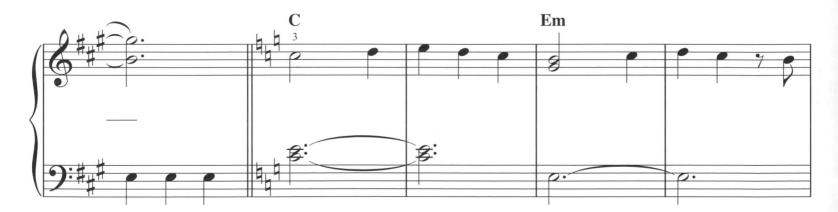

C   **Em**

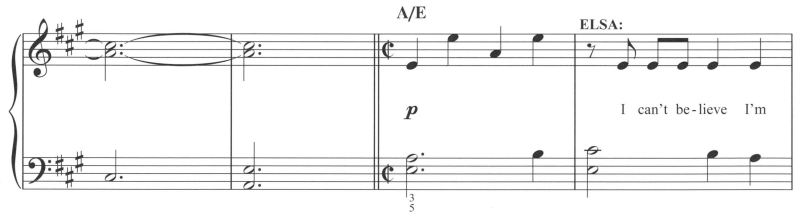

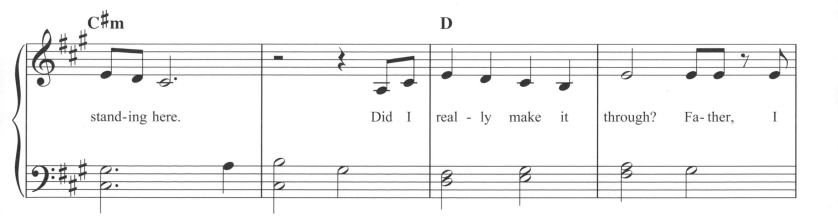

did it! Now what do I do? I can't stop smil - ing; how _

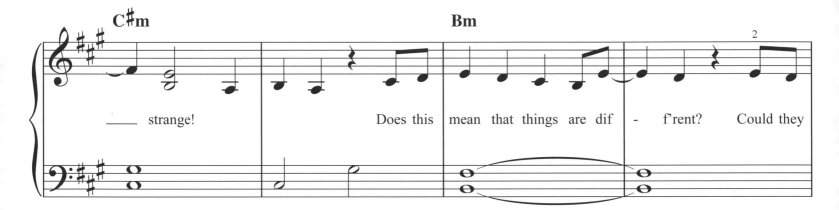

_ strange! Does this mean that things are dif - f'rent? Could they

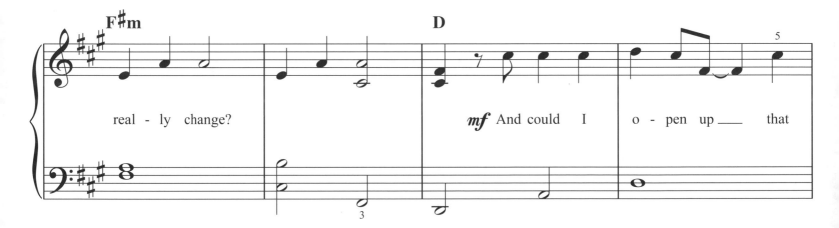

real - ly change? *mf* And could I o - pen up _ that

door and fi - n'lly see you face to face? I guess a queen can change the

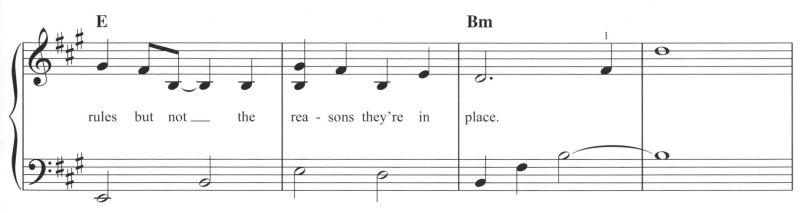

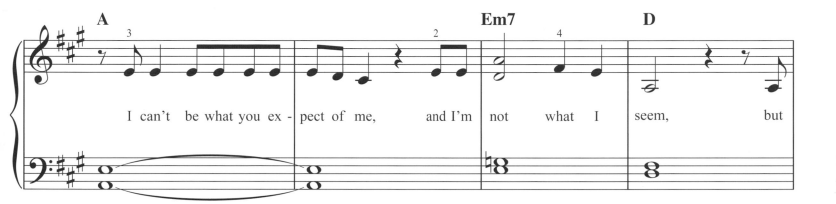

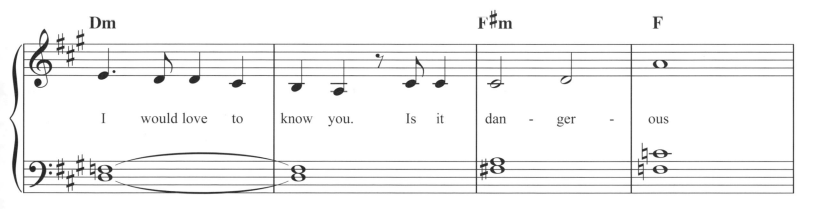

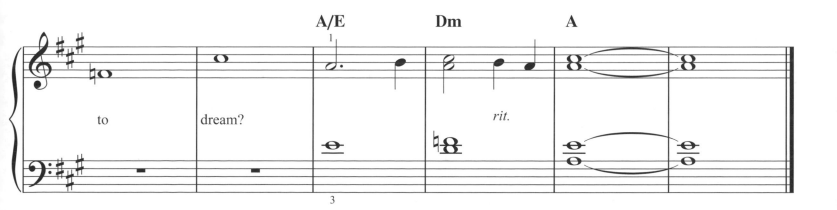

LOVE IS AN OPEN DOOR

Music and Lyrics by KRISTEN ANDERSON-LOPEZ
and ROBERT LOPEZ

Moderately slow

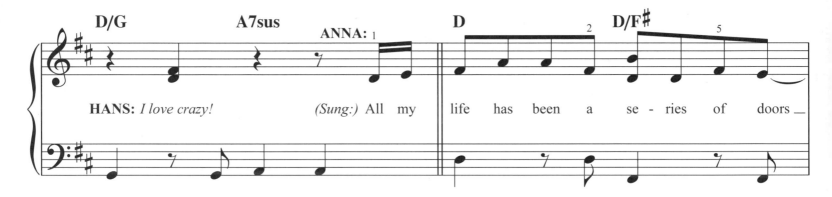

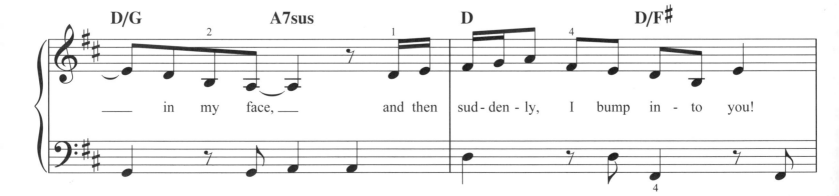

find my own place. ___ And may-be it's the par-ty talk-ing, or the

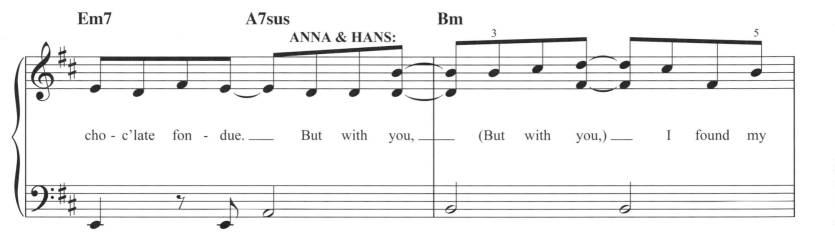

cho-c'late fon-due. ___ But with you, ___ (But with you,) ___ I found my

ANNA & HANS:

place, (I see your face.) and it's noth-ing like ___ I've ev-er known ___ be-

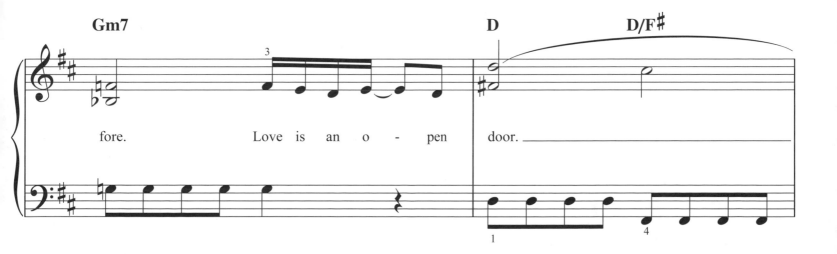

fore. Love is an o-pen door. ___

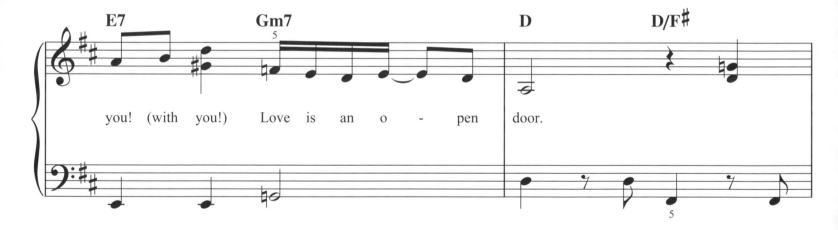

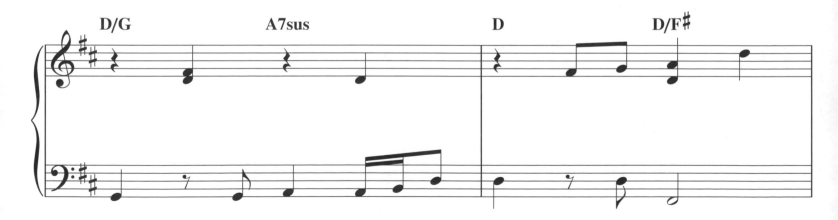

HANS: I mean, it's cra - zy! We fin - ish each oth - er's...

ANNA: (sand - wich - es!) **HANS:** *That's what I was gonna say!* **ANNA:** I nev - er **BOTH:** met some - one who thinks so much ___ like

me. *Jinx!* *Jinx a - gain!* Our men - tal syn - chro - ni - za - tion can

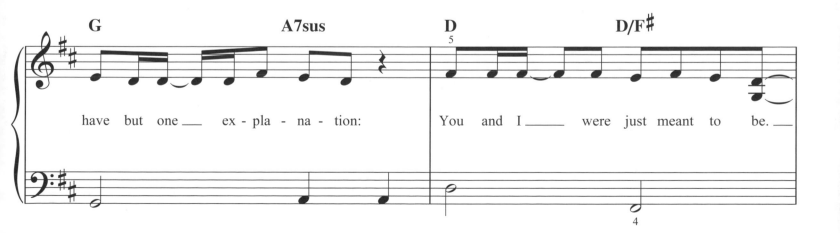

have but one ___ ex - pla - na - tion: You and I ___ were just meant to be. ___

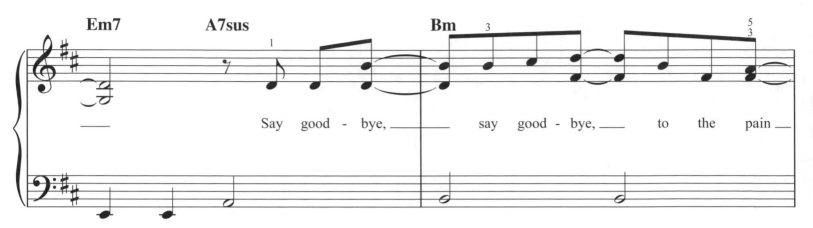

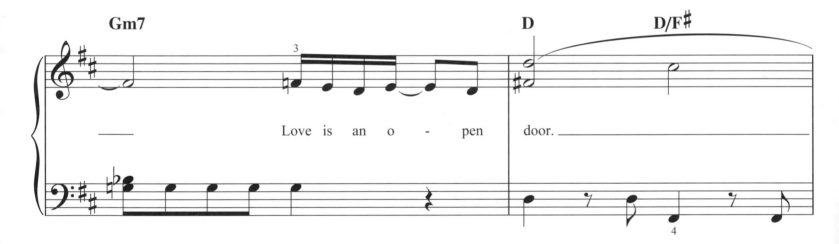

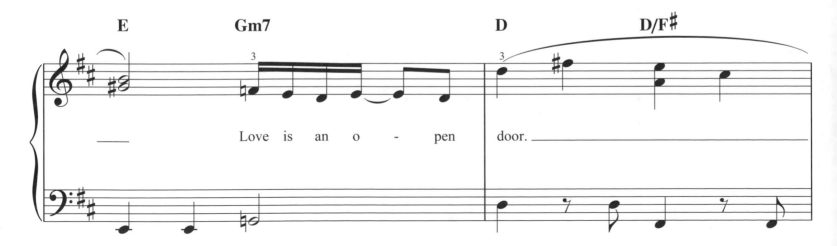

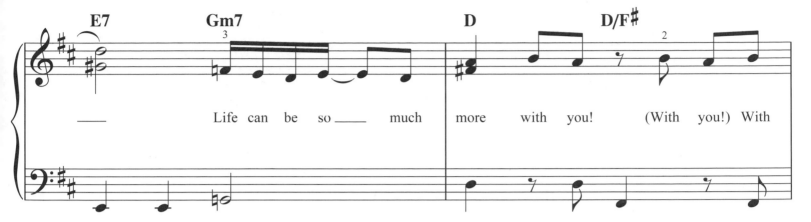

Life can be so ___ much more with you! (With you!) With

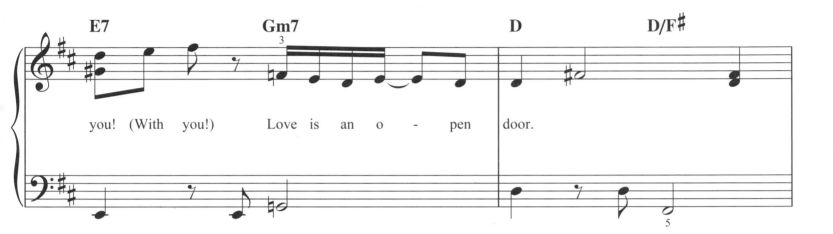

you! (With you!) Love is an o - pen door.

HANS: *(Spoken:) Can I say something crazy?* *Will you marry me?*

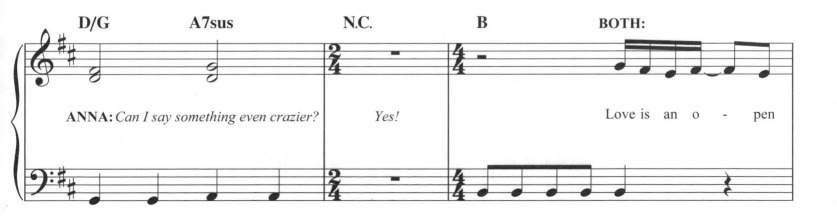

ANNA: *Can I say something even crazier?* *Yes!* Love is an o - pen

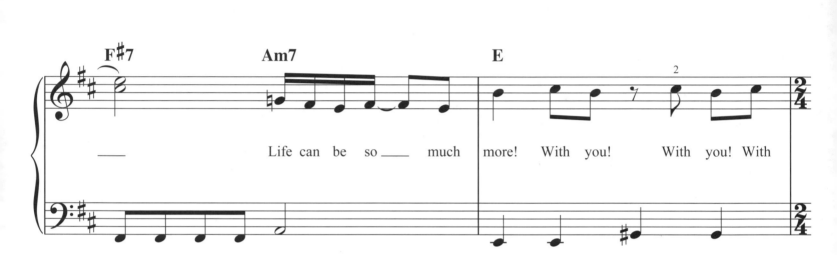

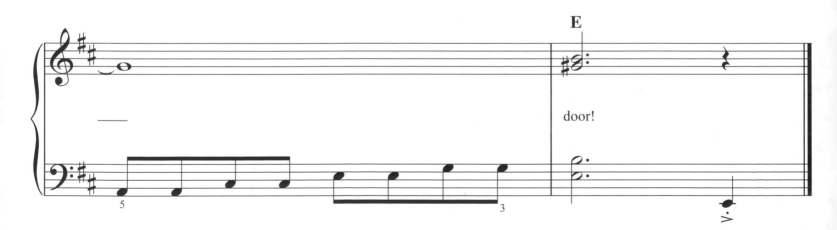

WHAT DO YOU KNOW ABOUT LOVE?

Music and Lyrics by KRISTEN ANDERSON-LOPEZ
and ROBERT LOPEZ

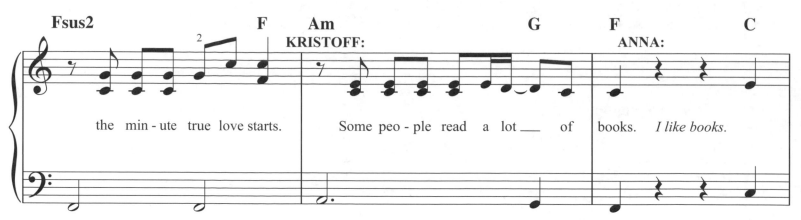

the min-ute true love starts.

KRISTOFF: Some peo-ple read a lot ___ of books. *I like books.*

Some peo-ple sim-ply know when true love says, "Hel-lo!" ___

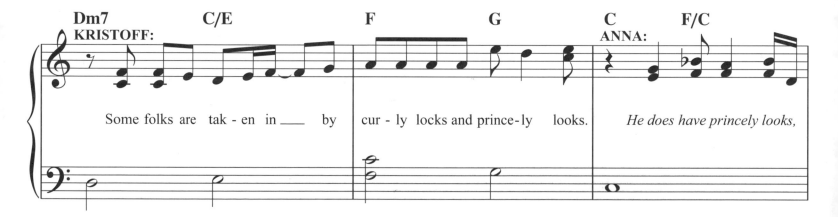

KRISTOFF: Some folks are tak-en in ___ by cur-ly locks and prince-ly looks. *He does have princely looks,*

we agree on that one! *Right! By the way, what color eyes does he have?*

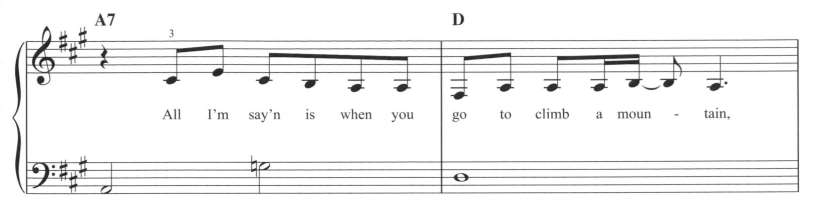

All I'm say'n is when you go to climb a moun-tain,

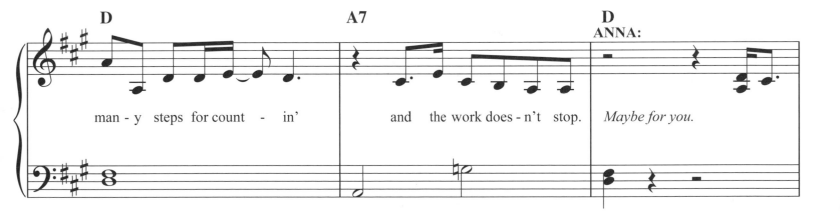

you don't just jump to the top. *If it's true love, you can!* There's scal - in' and scram - blin'and too

man - y steps for count - in' and the work does - n't stop. *Maybe for you.*

Love's not an eas - y climb, you have to take your time. We get a whole life, ___ that's the plan. ___

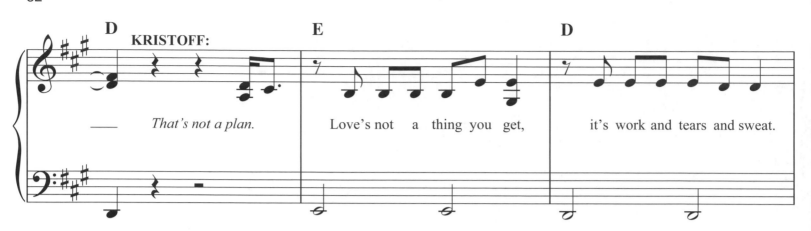

KRISTOFF:
That's not a plan. Love's not a thing you get, it's work and tears and sweat.

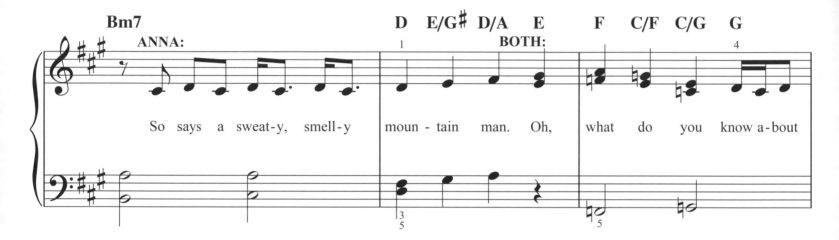

ANNA:
So says a sweat-y, smell-y moun-tain man. Oh, **BOTH:** what do you know a-bout

love? What do you know a-bout love?

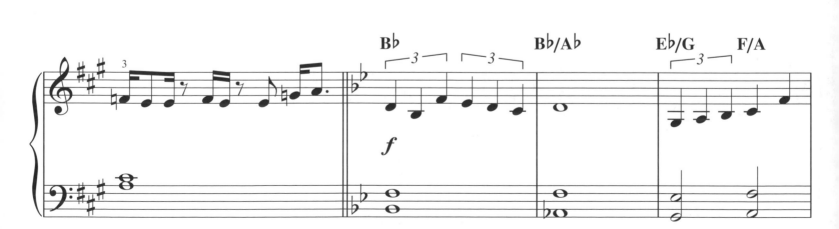

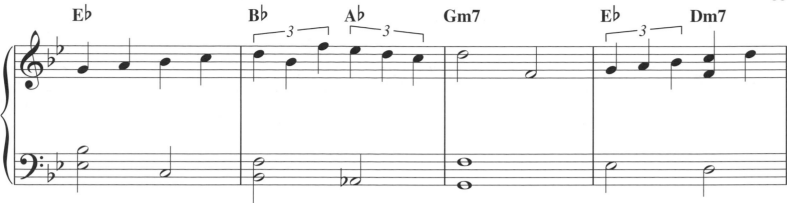

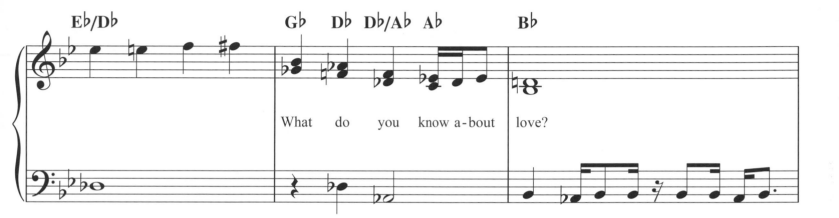

What do you know a-bout love?

What do you know a - bout love?

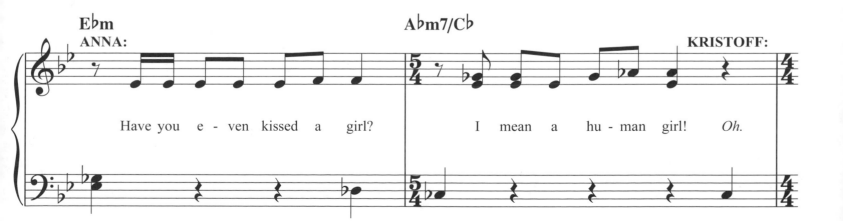

ANNA: Have you e - ven kissed a girl? I mean a hu - man girl! *Oh.* **KRISTOFF:**

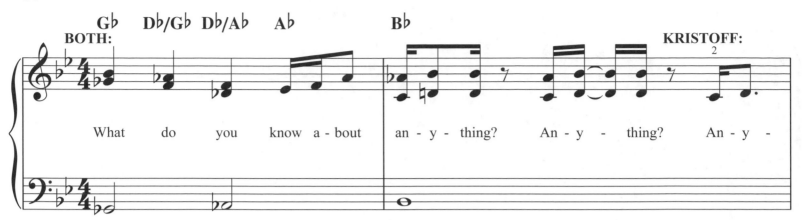

Gb   Db/Gb Db/Ab   Ab   Bb

BOTH: KRISTOFF:

What do you know a-bout an-y-thing? An-y - thing? An-y -

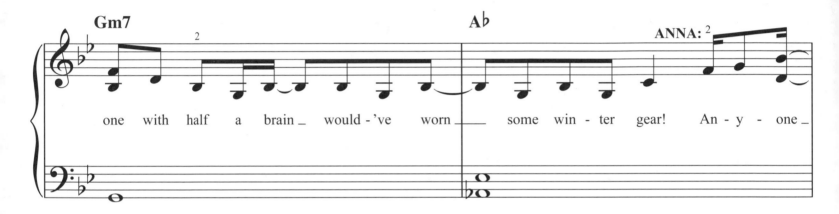

Gm7   Ab

ANNA:

one with half a brain would-'ve worn some win-ter gear! An-y-one

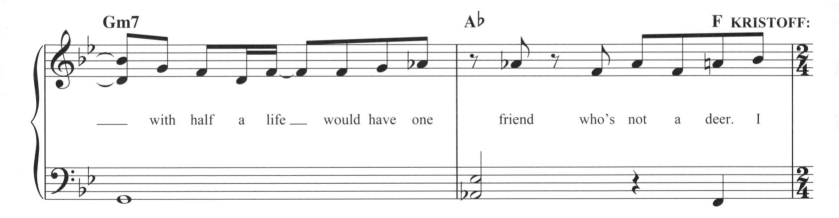

Gm7   Ab   F KRISTOFF:

with half a life would have one friend who's not a deer. I

Bb   Gm7

do. An-y fool who jumps head-long is gon-

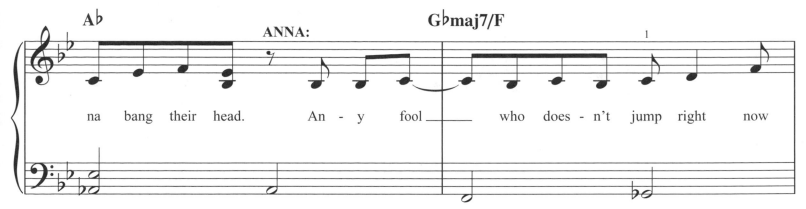

na bang their head. An-y fool who does-n't jump right now

is prob-'ly gon-na end up dead! *Aaah!* Like I said.

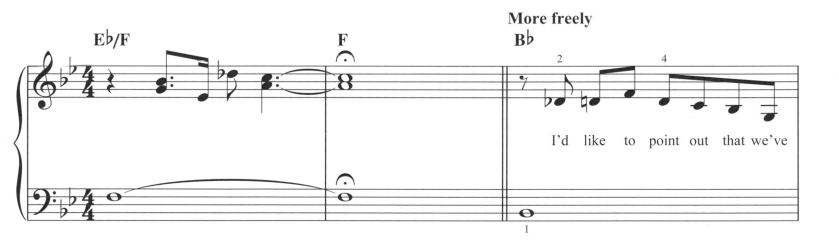

I'd like to point out that we've

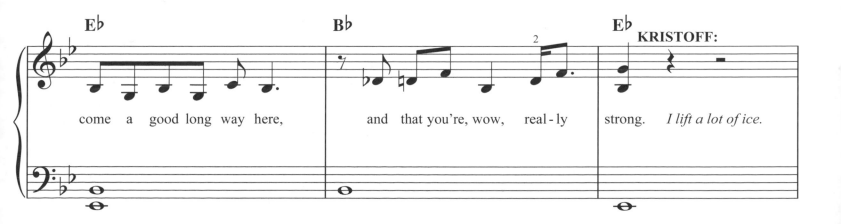

come a good long way here, and that you're, wow, real-ly strong. *I lift a lot of ice.*

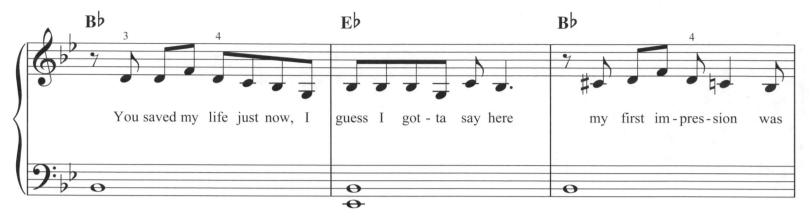

You saved my life just now, I guess I got-ta say here my first im-pres-sion was

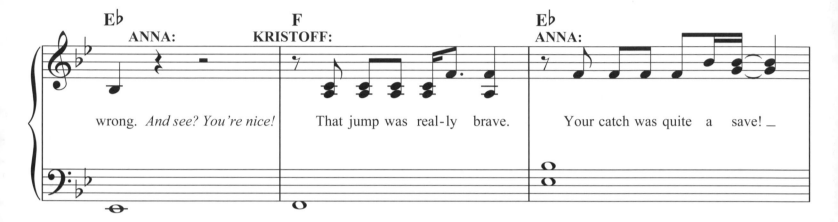

ANNA: KRISTOFF: ANNA:

wrong. *And see? You're nice!* That jump was real-ly brave. Your catch was quite a save! _

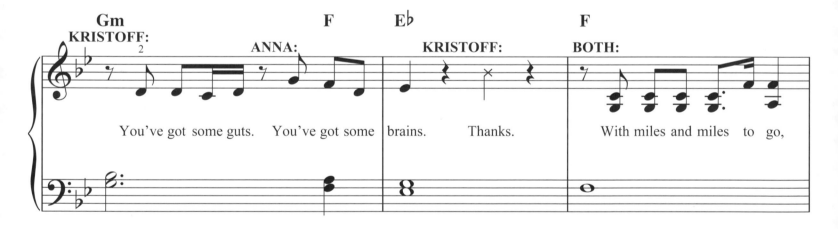

KRISTOFF: ANNA: KRISTOFF: BOTH:

You've got some guts. You've got some brains. Thanks. With miles and miles to go,

I guess it's nice to know _ that I _ can trust you. Though the ques-tion still re-mains. _

Moving into tempo

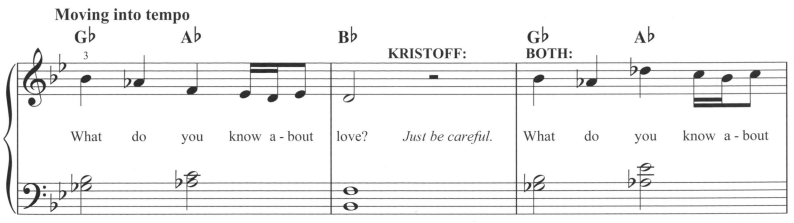

What do you know a - bout love? *Just be careful.* What do you know a - bout

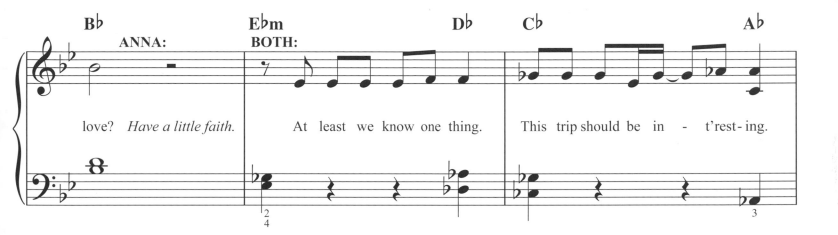

love? *Have a little faith.* At least we know one thing. This trip should be in - t'rest-ing.

What do you know a-bout love? What do

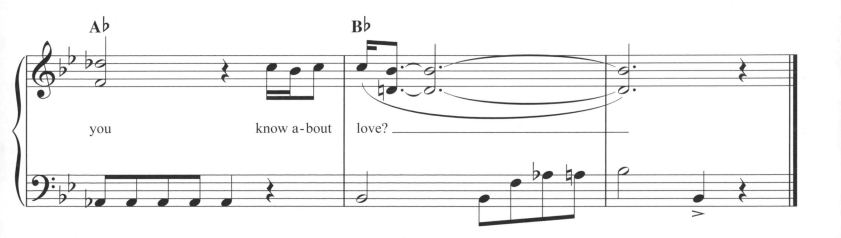

you know a-bout love? _____

IN SUMMER

Music and Lyrics by KRISTEN ANDERSON-LOPEZ
and ROBERT LOPEZ

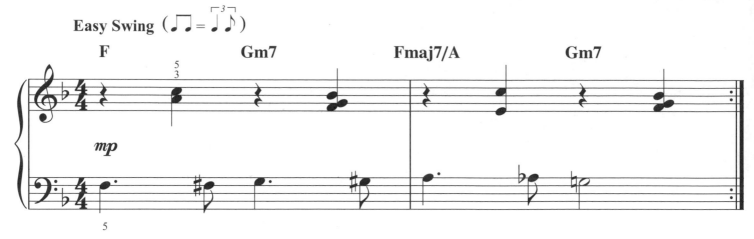

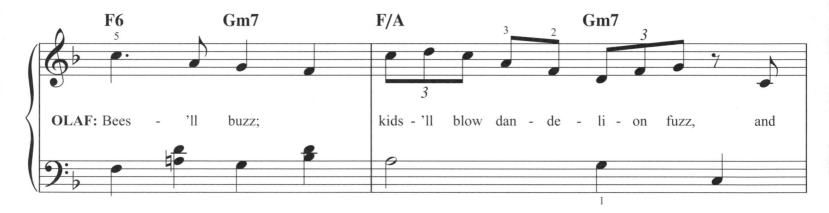

OLAF: Bees - 'll buzz; kids - 'll blow dan - de - li - on fuzz, and

I'll be do - ing what - ev - er snow does in sum - mer.

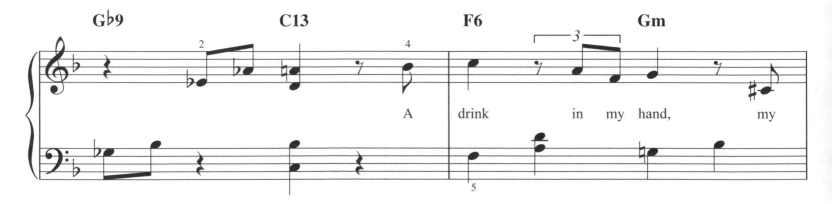

A drink in my hand, my

snow up a-gainst the burn-ing sand, ___ prob-'ly get-ting gor-geous-ly tanned in

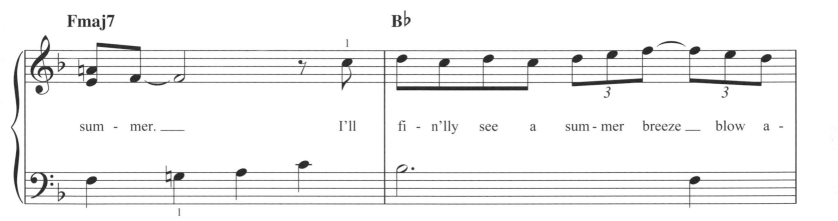

sum - mer. ___ I'll fi - n'lly see a sum-mer breeze ___ blow a-

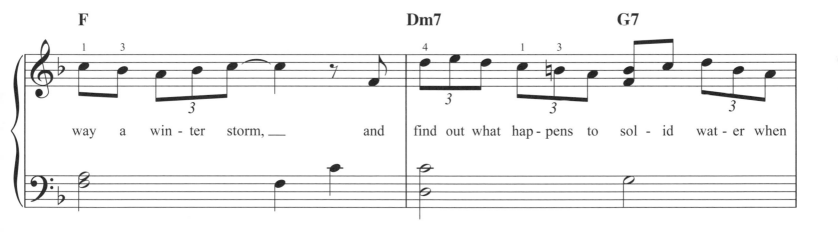

way a win-ter storm, ___ and find out what hap-pens to sol-id wat-er when

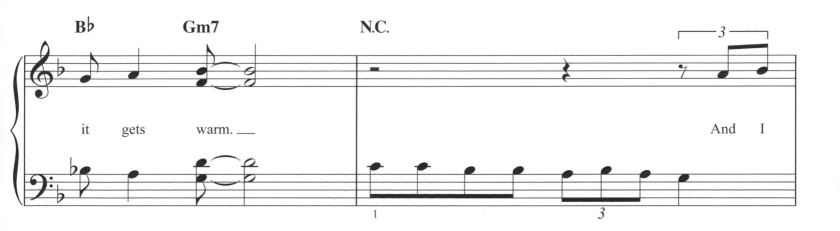

it gets warm. ___ And I

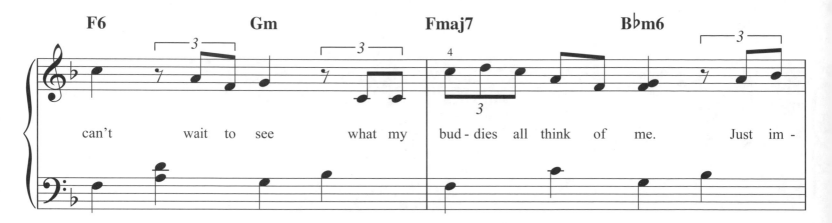

can't   wait   to   see   what my   bud - dies all think of   me.   Just im -

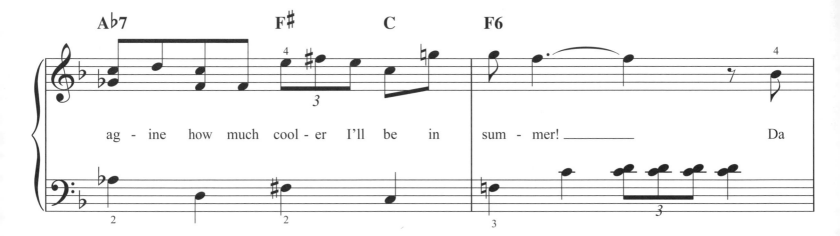

ag - ine   how much cool - er I'll be   in   sum - mer! _____   Da

da,   da   doo,   a   ba   ba   ba   ba   ba boo. ___   The

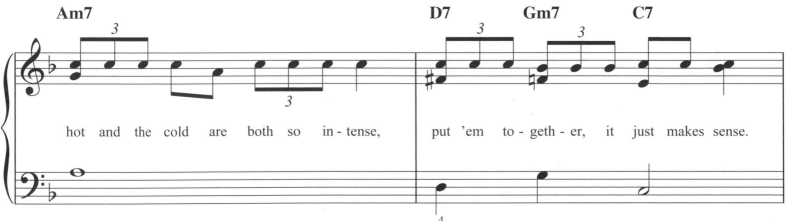

hot   and the cold are both so in - tense,   put 'em to - geth - er, it   just makes sense.

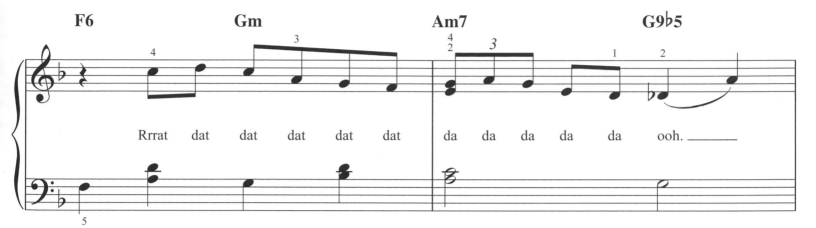

F6   **Gm**   **Am7**   **G9♭5**

Rrrat dat dat dat dat dat da da da da da ooh. _____

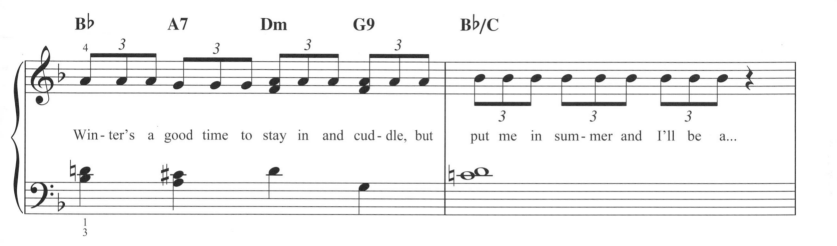

B♭   **A7**   **Dm**   **G9**   **B♭/C**

Win - ter's a good time to stay in and cud - dle, but put me in sum - mer and I'll be a...

N.C.   **B♭6**

(Spoken:) happy snowman!   *(Sung:)* When life gets rough, I like to

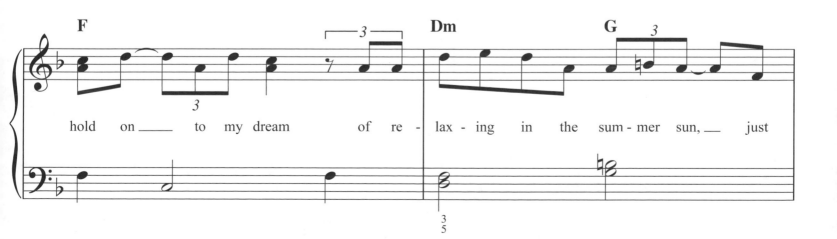

F   **Dm**   **G**

hold on _____ to my dream of re - lax - ing in the sum - mer sun, _____ just

let - tin' off   steam. ___   Oh, the   sky   will be blue,   and

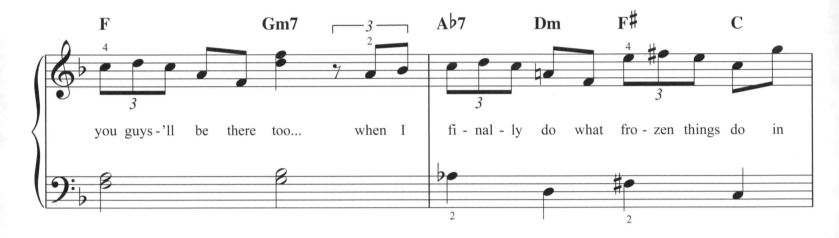

you guys -'ll   be   there   too...   when I   fi - nal - ly   do   what   fro - zen things   do   in

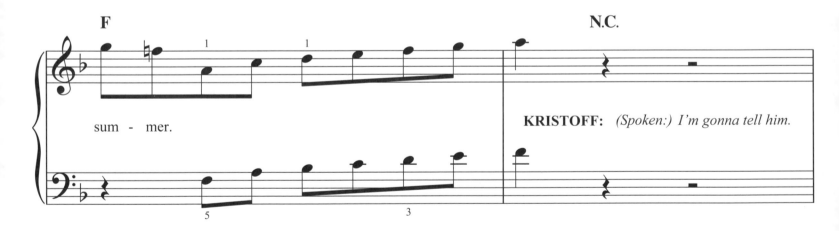

sum - mer.   **KRISTOFF:** *(Spoken:) I'm gonna tell him.*

ANNA: *Don't you dare!*   **OLAF:** In   sum - mer! _____

HANS OF THE SOUTHERN ISLES
(Reprise)

Music and Lyrics by KRISTEN ANDERSON-LOPEZ
and ROBERT LOPEZ

Moderately, with dignity

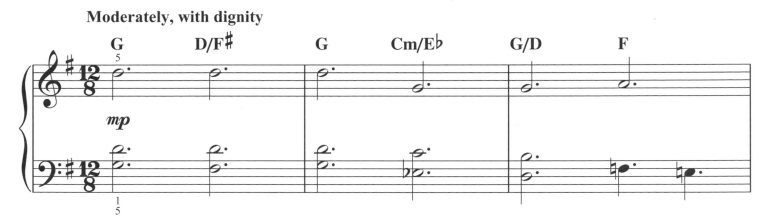

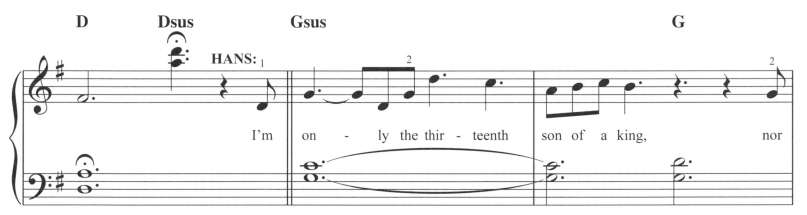

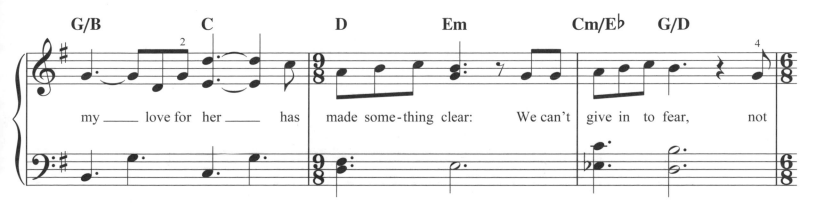

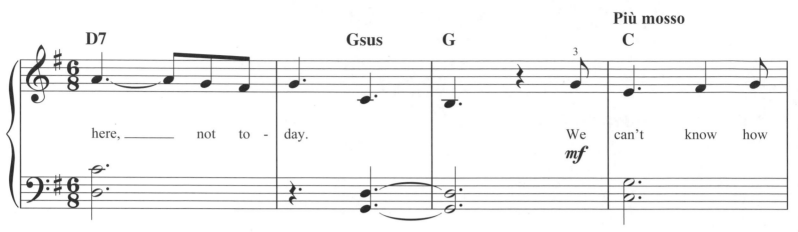

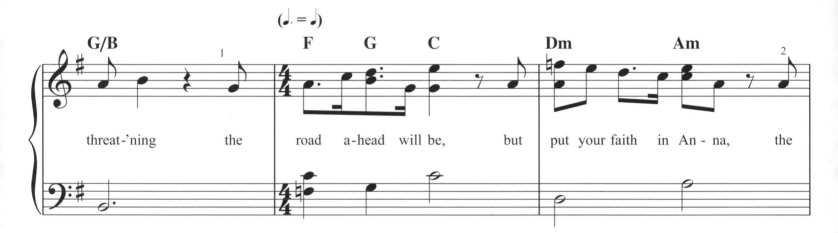

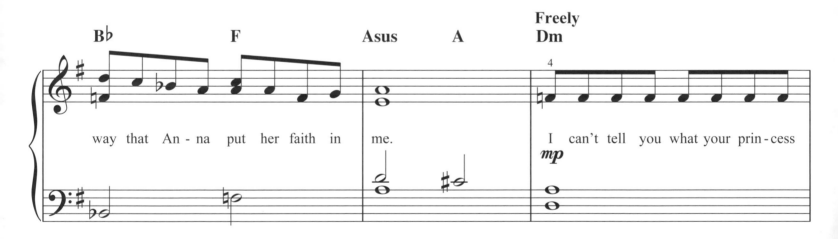

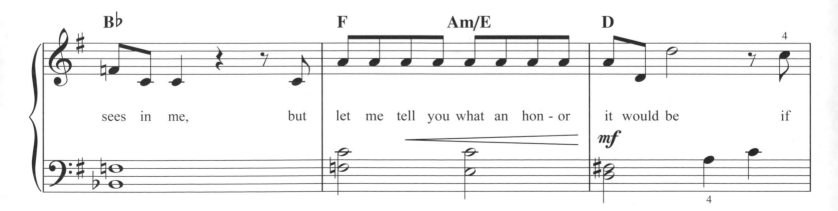

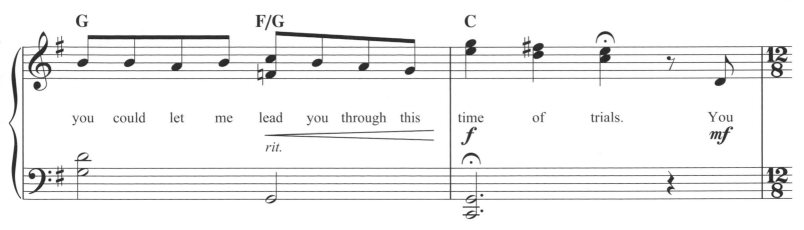

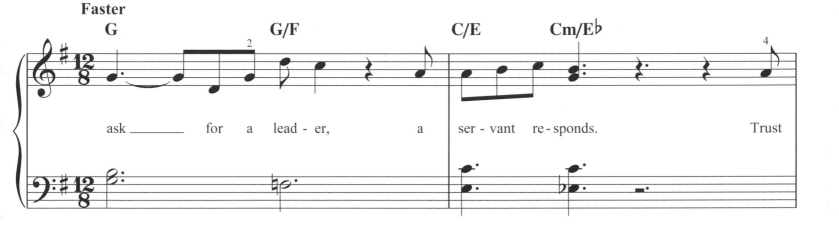

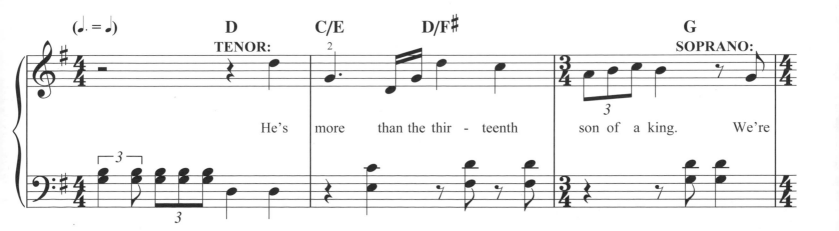

66

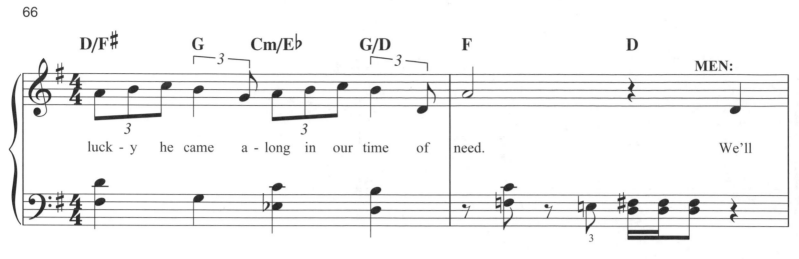

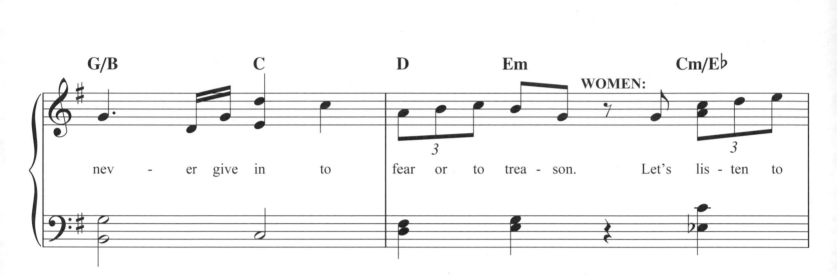

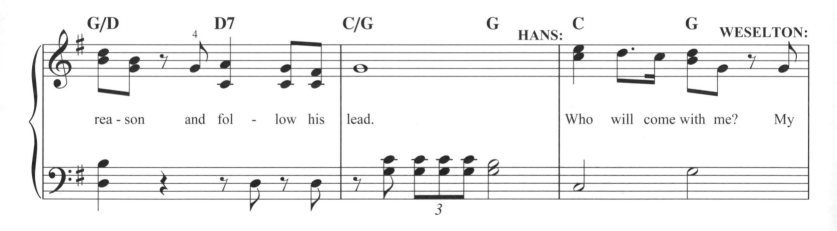

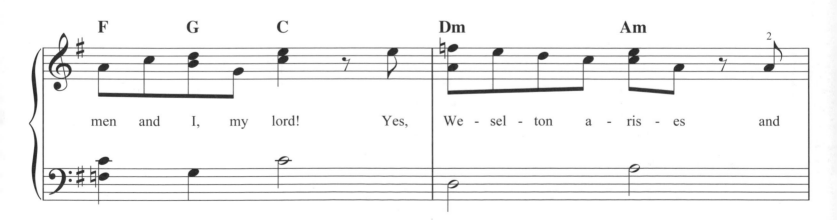

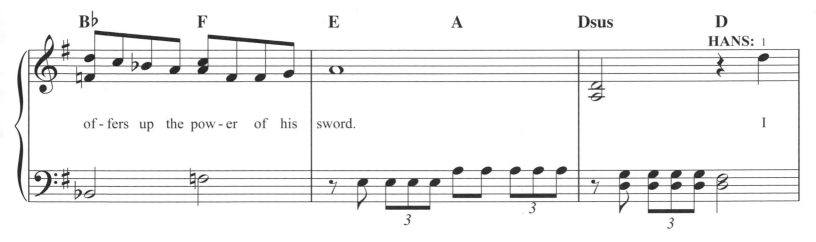

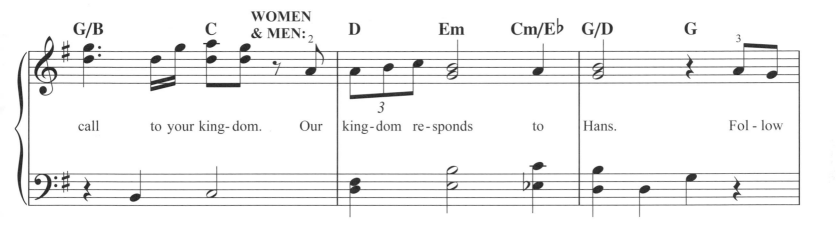

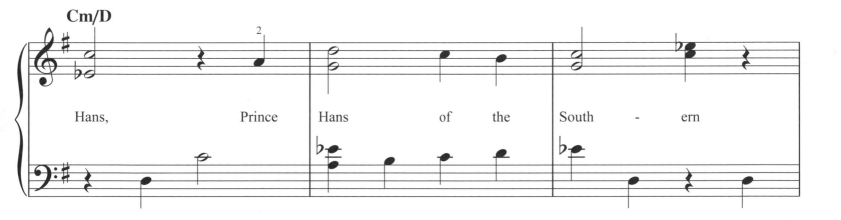

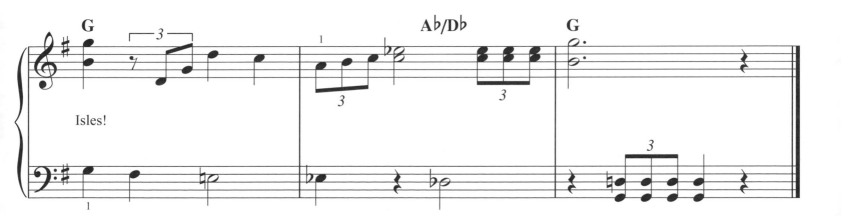

LET IT GO

Music and Lyrics by KRISTEN ANDERSON-LOPEZ
and ROBERT LOPEZ

Half-time feel, mysterious

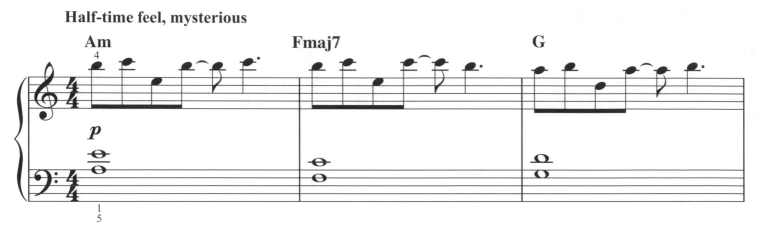

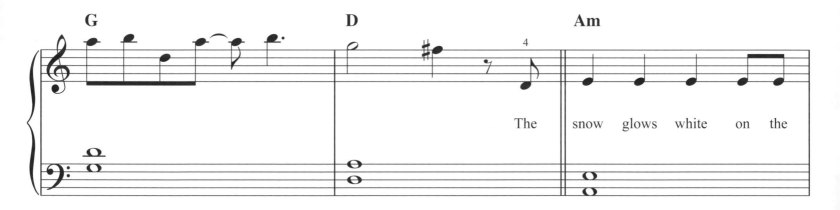

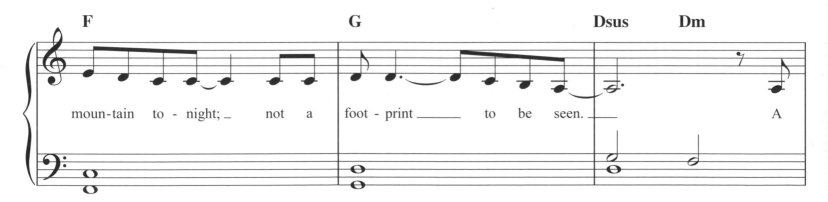

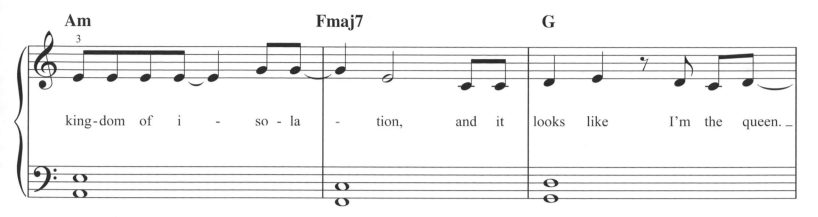

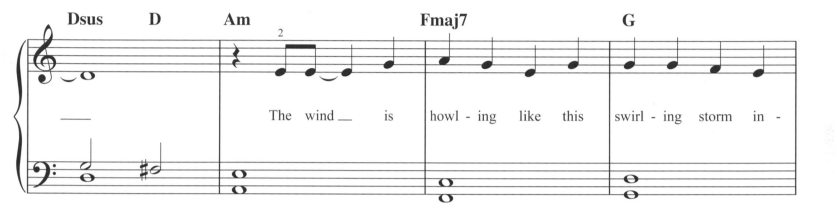

see; be the good girl you al - ways have to be. Con - ceal, _ don't

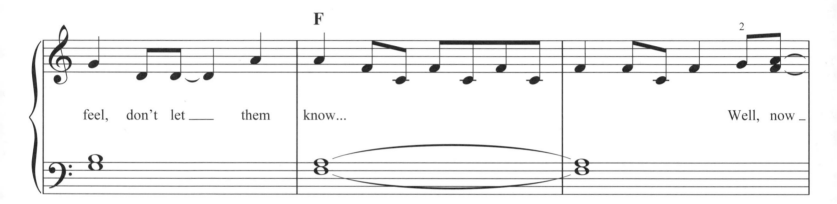

feel, don't let _ them know... Well, now _

_ they know. _ Let it go, _ let it go; _

_ can't _ hold it back an - y - more. _ Let it go, _
_ I am one with the wind and sky. _ Let it go, _

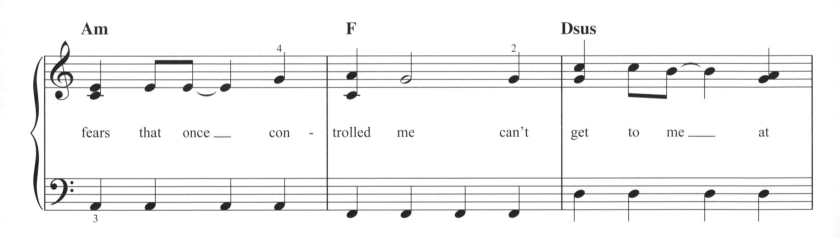

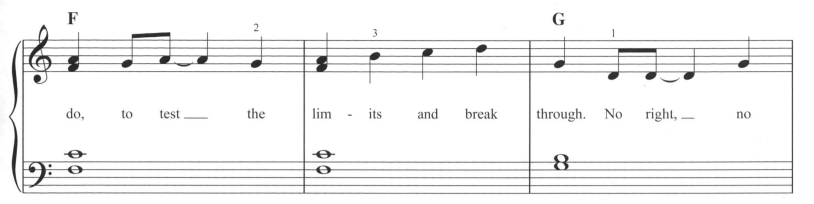

do, to test ___ the lim - its and break through. No right, ___ no

wrong, no rules for me, ___ I'm free!

D.S. al Coda

Let it go, ___

CODA

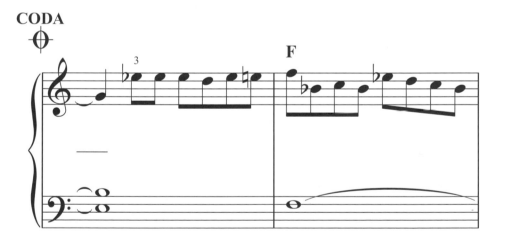

___

My pow - er flur - ries through the air in - to the

ground. My soul __ is spi - ral - ing in

fro - zen frac - tals all a - round. __ And one __ thought

cry - stal - liz - es like an i - cy blast:

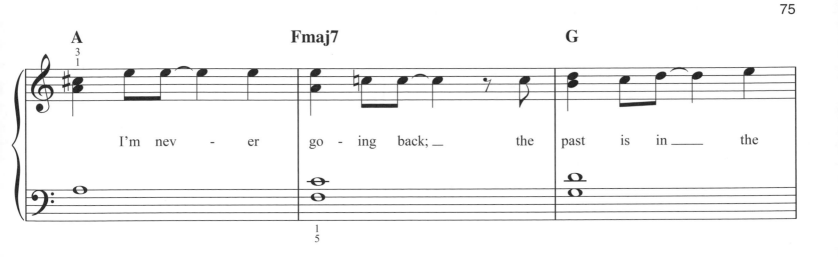

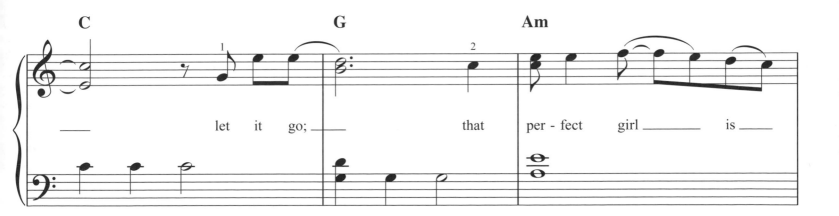

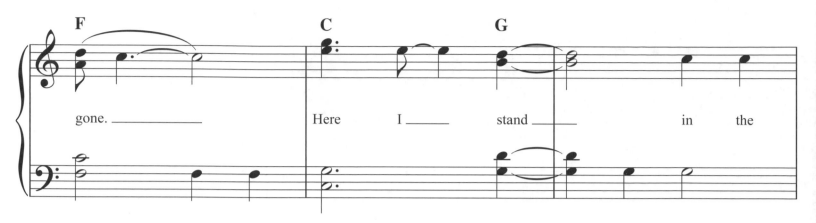

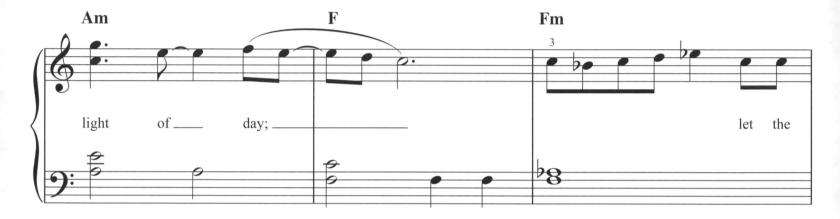

HYGGE

Music and Lyrics by KRISTEN ANDERSON-LOPEZ
and ROBERT LOPEZ

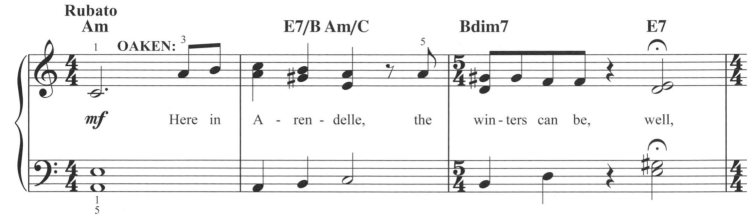

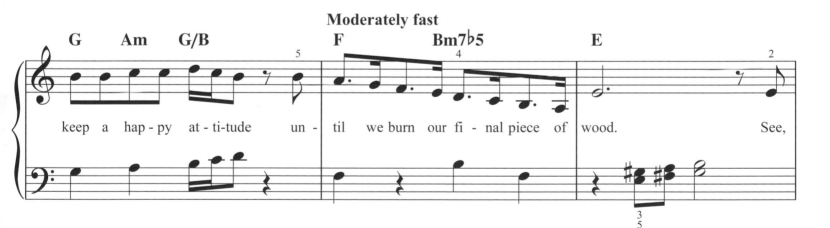

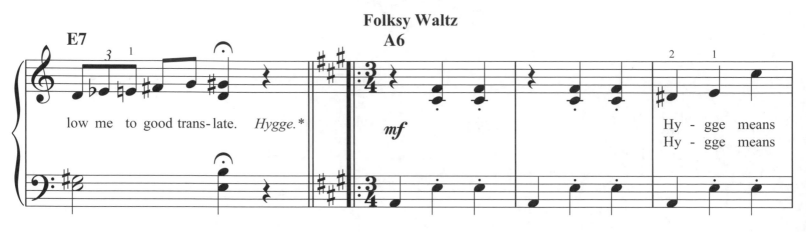

Folksy Waltz

low me to good trans-late. *Hygge.**

Hy - gge means
Hy - gge means

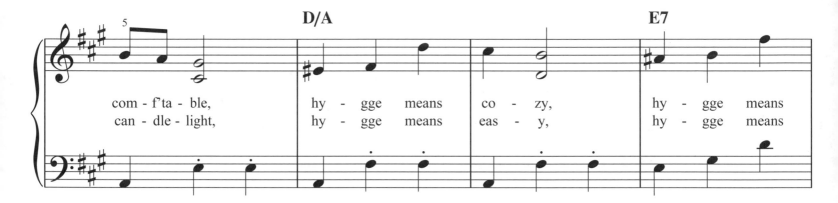

com - f'ta - ble,
can - dle - light,

hy - gge means
hy - gge means

co - zy,
eas - y,

hy - gge means
hy - gge means

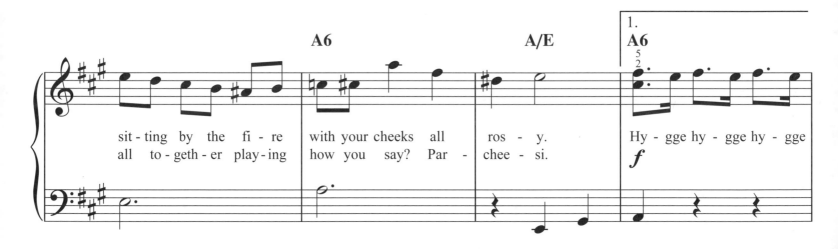

sit - ting by the fi - re
all to - geth - er play-ing

with your cheeks all
how you say? Par -

ros - y.
chee - si.

Hy - gge hy - gge hy - gge

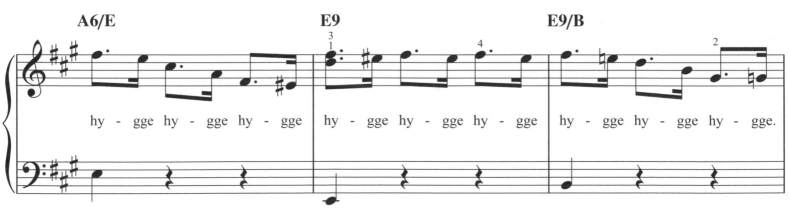

hy - gge hy - gge hy - gge

hy - gge hy - gge hy - gge

hy - gge hy - gge hy - gge.

*Pronounced "hue-gah"

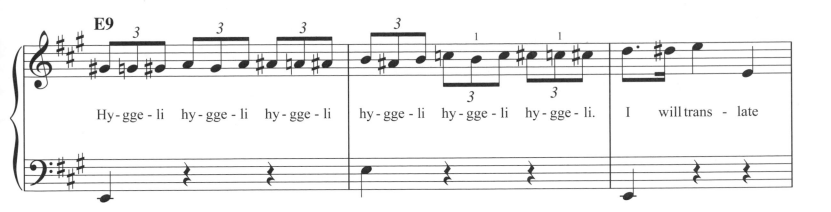

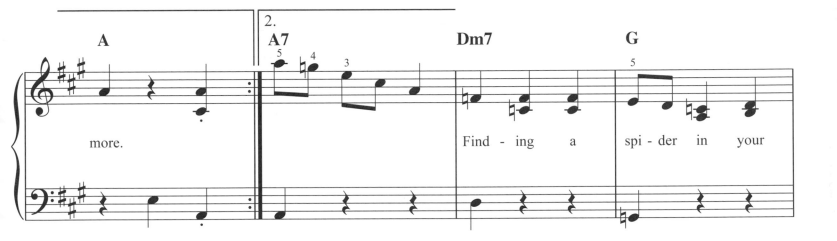

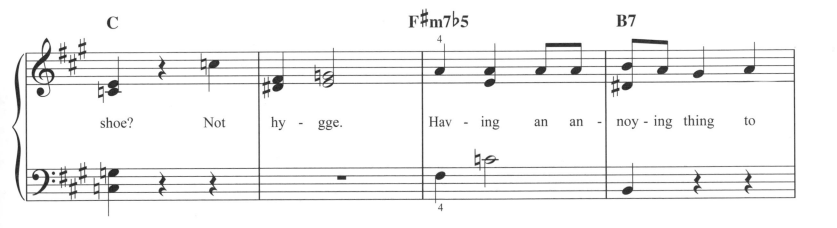

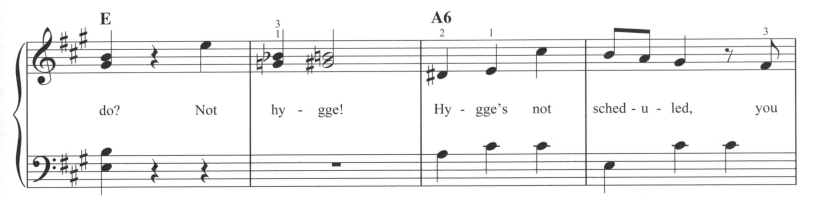

80

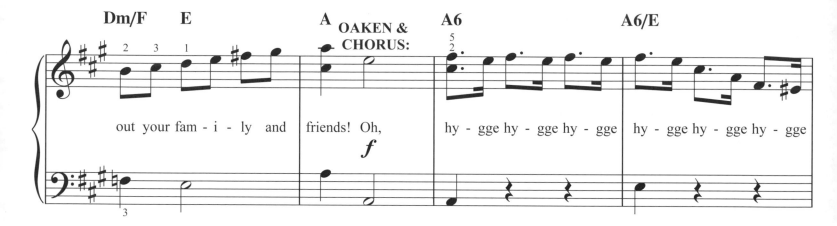

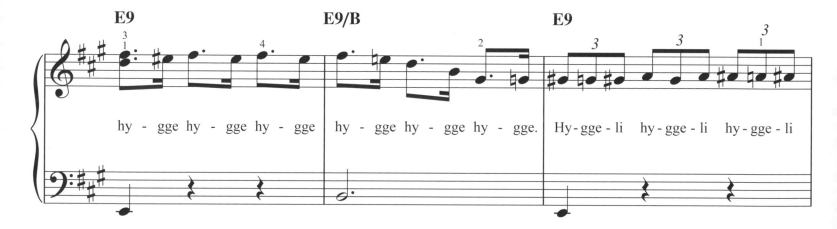

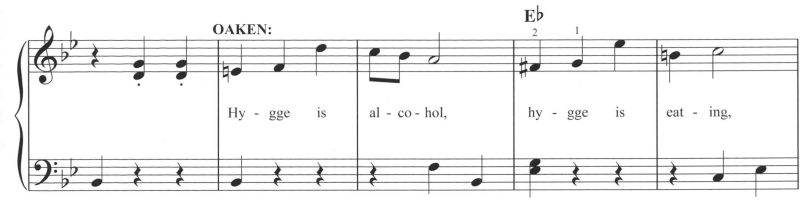

OAKEN:

Hy - gge is al - co - hol, hy - gge is eat - ing,

hy - gge is glugg, a - maz - ing stuff when you are need - ing heat - ing.

Hy - gge means you're friend - ly. You stop want - ing to be rude.

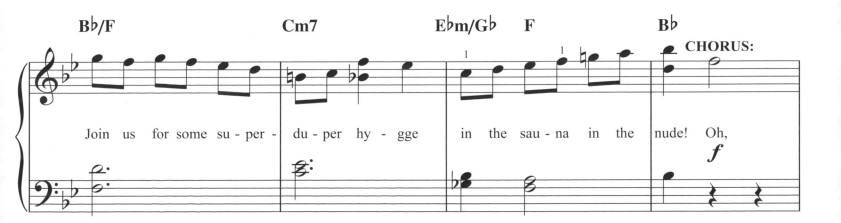

Join us for some su - per - du - per hy - gge in the sau - na in the nude! Oh,

CHORUS:

82

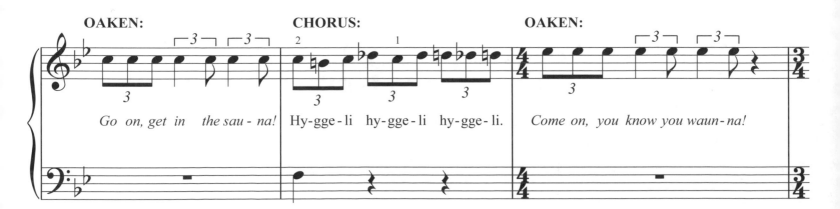

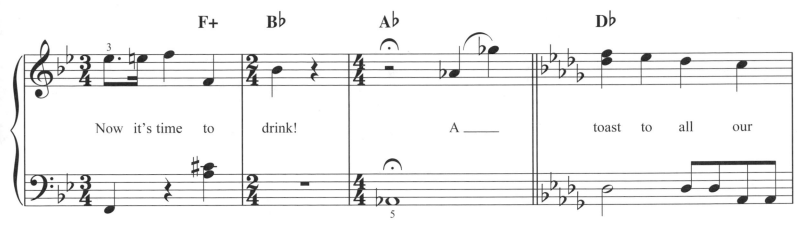

Now it's time to drink! A _____ toast to all our

fam - i - ly and friends; to hy - gge in a storm that nev - er ends. So

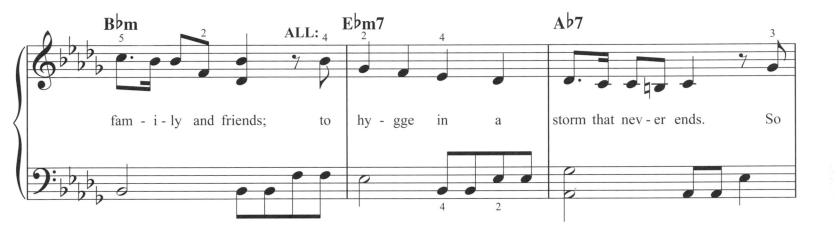

let it keep on go - ing; we al - ways have each oth - er. The glugg is brewed, we're here, we're nude, and

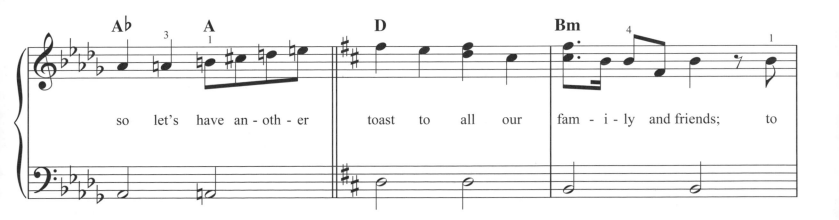

so let's have an - oth - er toast to all our fam - i - ly and friends; to

hy - gge in a storm that nev - er ends. So let it keep on go - ing. We

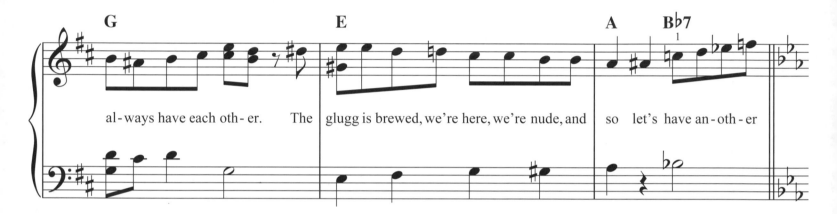

al - ways have each oth - er. The glugg is brewed, we're here, we're nude, and so let's have an - oth - er

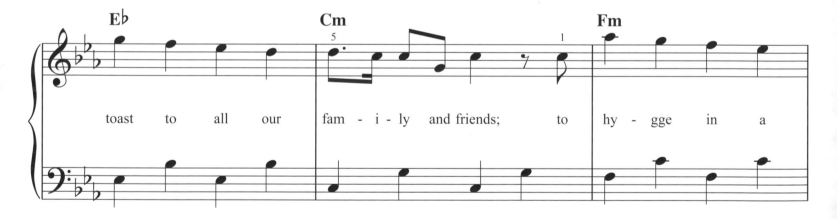

toast to all our fam - i - ly and friends; to hy - gge in a

storm that nev - er ends. So let it keep on go - ing; we al - ways have each oth - er. The

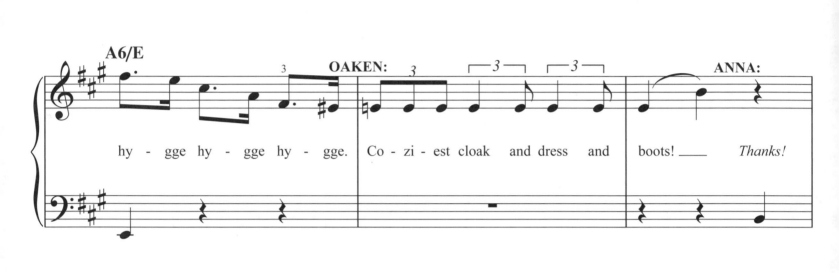

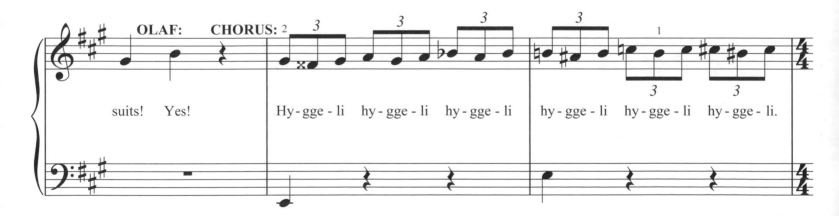

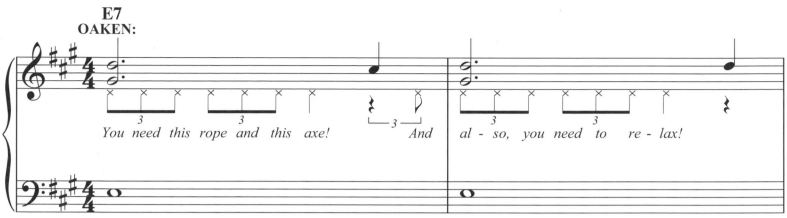

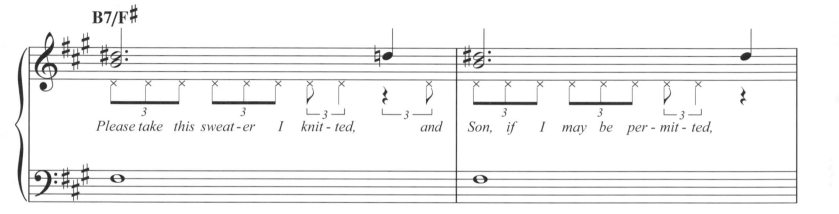

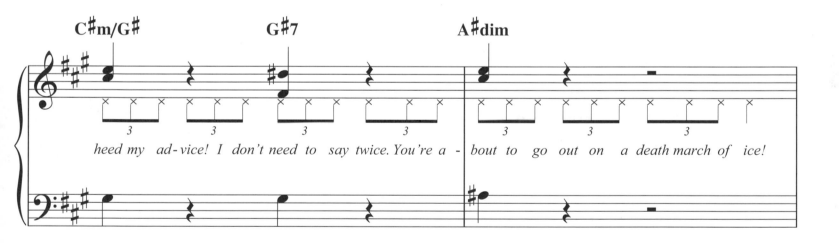

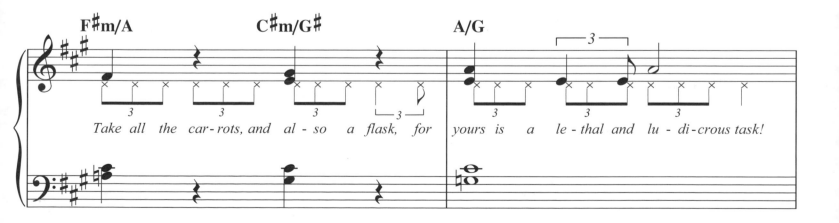

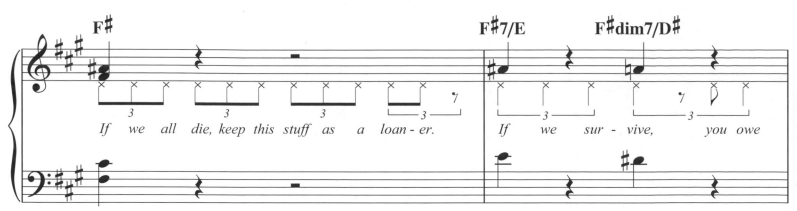

F#

If we all die, keep this stuff as a loan-er.

F#7/E   **F#dim7/D#**

If we sur-vive, you owe

F#7

OLAF:

ten thou-sand kro-ner. Deal!

Broadly (♩♩ = ♩♪)
B6
CHORUS:

Hy - gge   hy - gge

f

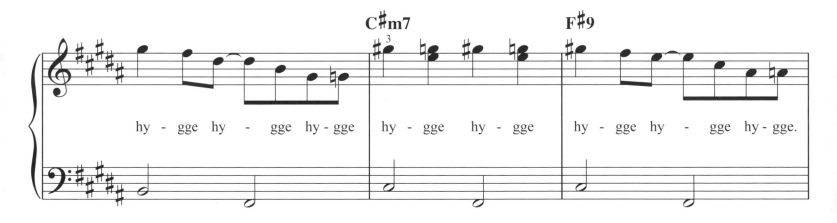

hy - gge hy - gge hy - gge

C#m7

hy - gge   hy - gge

F#9

hy - gge hy - gge hy - gge.

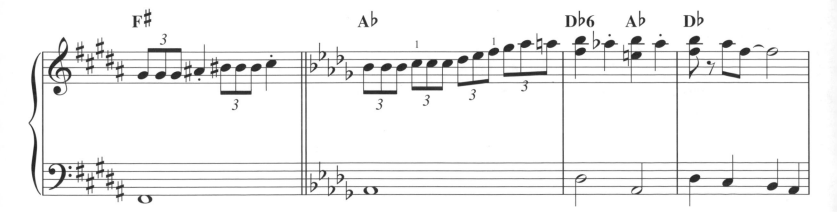

F#

Ab

Db6   **Ab**   **Db**

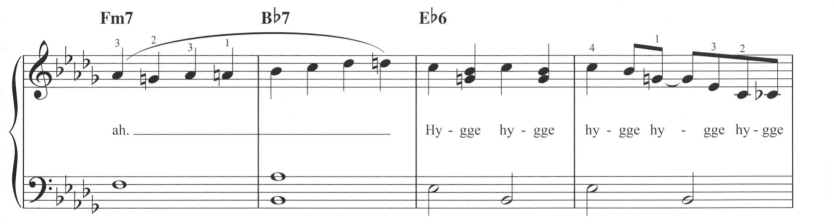

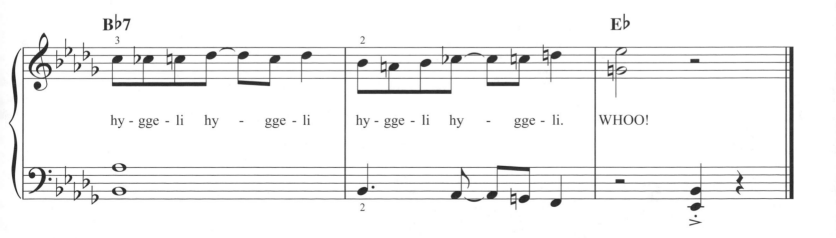

FIXER UPPER

(Broadway Version)

Music and Lyrics by KRISTEN ANDERSON-LOPEZ
and ROBERT LOPEZ

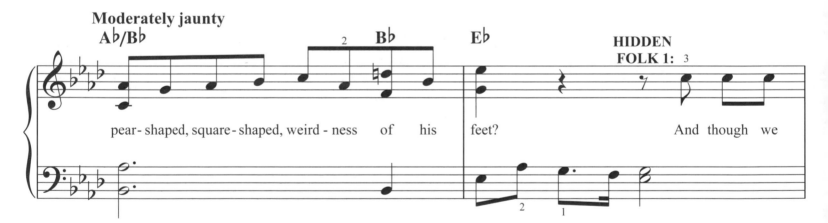

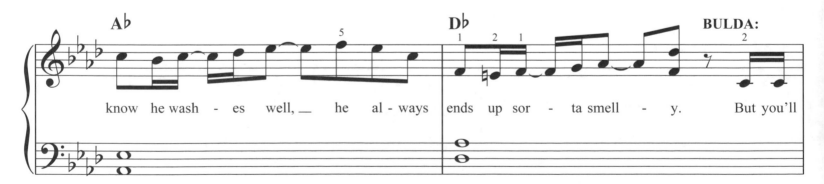

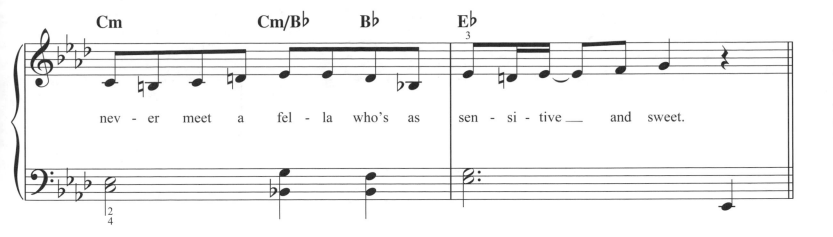

never meet a fel-la who's as sen-si-tive____ and sweet.

PABBIE: So he's a bit of a fix-er up-per, so he's got____ a few flaws. **BULDA:** Like his pe-

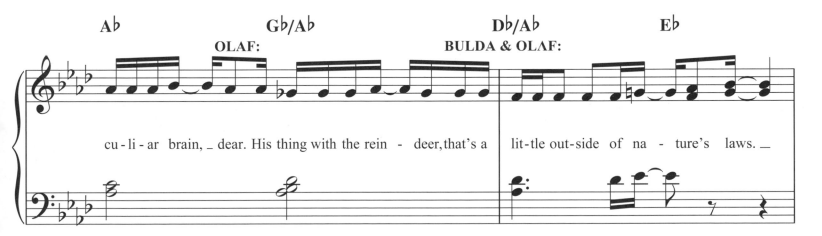

OLAF: cu-li-ar brain,_ dear. His thing with the rein-deer, that's a **BULDA & OLAF:** lit-tle out-side of na-ture's laws.____

PABBIE: So he's a bit of a fix-er up-per, but this we're cer-tain of:_____ **BULDA:** you can

fix this fix-er up-per up with a lit-tle bit ___ of love. ___ Na na ___ na hei a na.

Na na ___ na hei ja nah hi ___ ja na. ___ Is it the

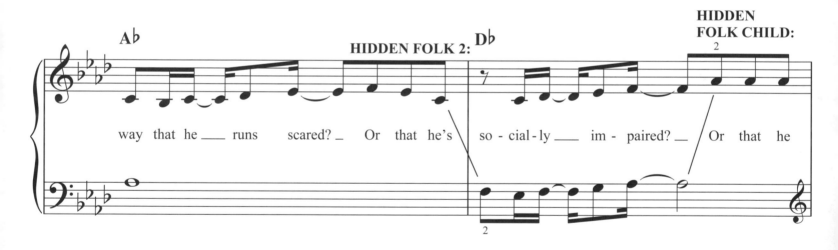

way that he ___ runs scared? ___ Or that he's so-cial-ly ___ im-paired? ___ Or that he

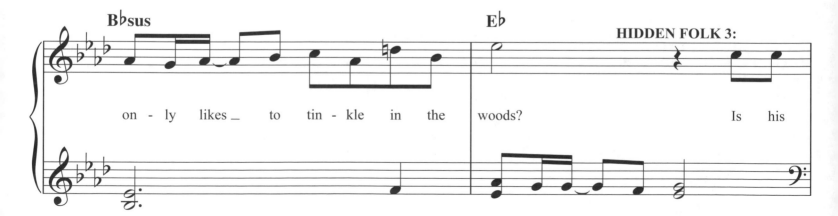

on-ly likes ___ to tin-kle in the woods? Is his

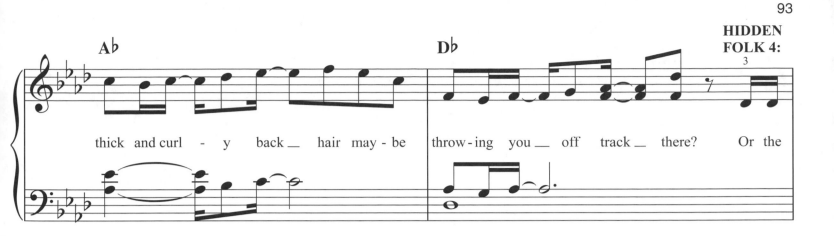

A♭   D♭

thick and curl - y back __ hair may - be throw-ing you __ off track __ there? Or the

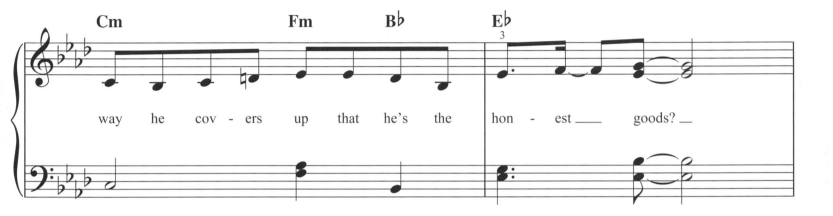

Cm   Fm   B♭   E♭

way he cov - ers up that he's the hon - est __ goods? __

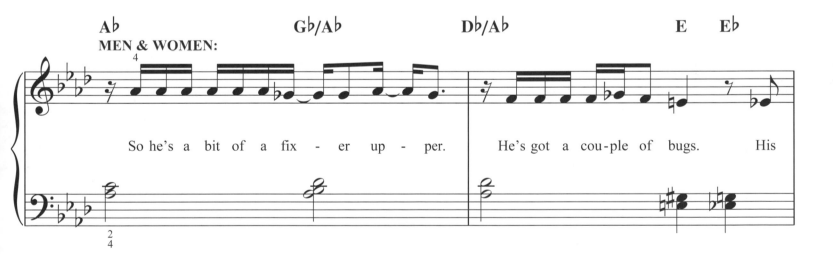

A♭   G♭/A♭   D♭/A♭   E   E♭

MEN & WOMEN:

So he's a bit of a fix - er up - per. He's got a cou-ple of bugs. His

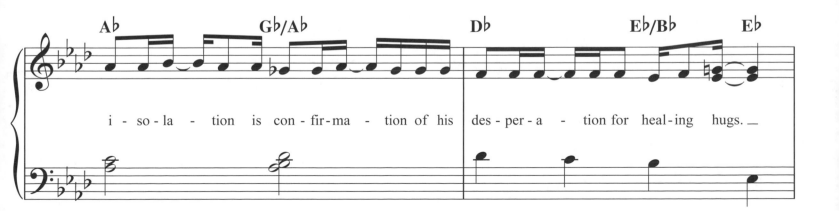

A♭   G♭/A♭   D♭   E♭/B♭   E♭

i - so - la - tion is con - fir-ma - tion of his des - per - a - tion for heal-ing hugs. __

He's just a bit of a fix - er up - per, but we know what to do. _____ The

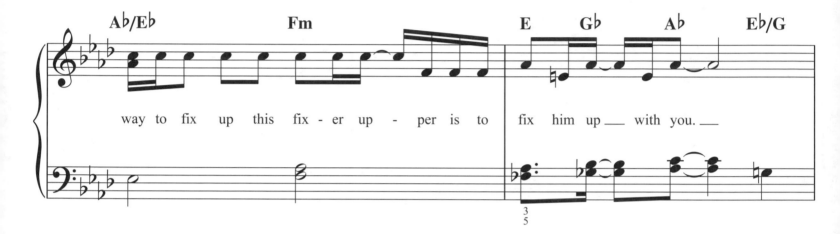

way to fix up this fix - er up - per is to fix him up ___ with you. ___

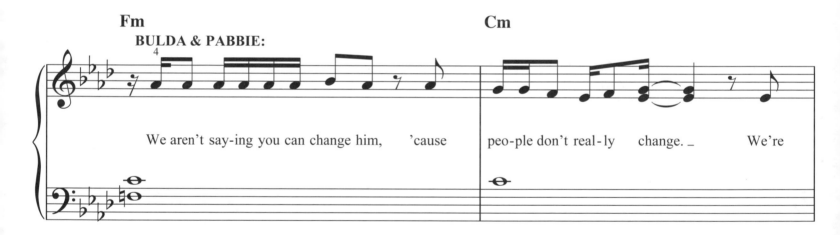

BULDA & PABBIE:

We aren't say-ing you can change him, 'cause peo-ple don't real-ly change. ___ We're

on - ly say - ing that love's a force that's pow-er-ful ___ and strange.

Hu-mans make __ bad choic-es if they're mad or scared __ or stressed. __ But

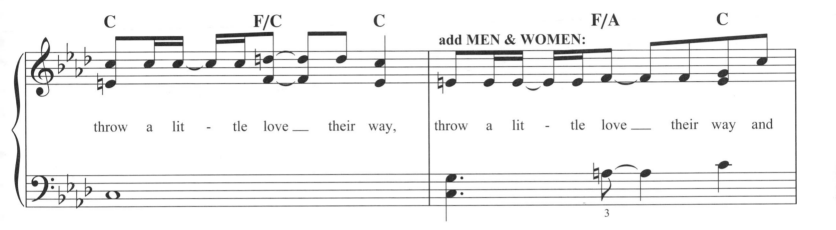

throw a lit - tle love __ their way, throw a lit - tle love __ their way and

add MEN & WOMEN:

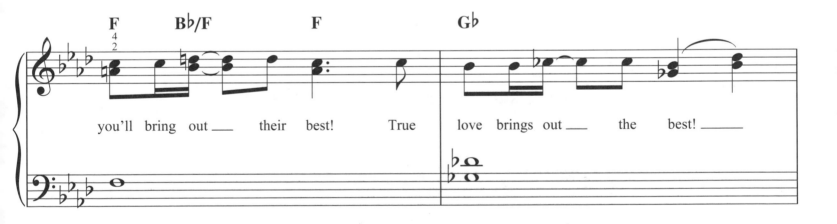

you'll bring out __ their best! True love brings out __ the best! _____

MEN & WOMEN:

Ev-'ry-one's a bit of a fix - er up - per,

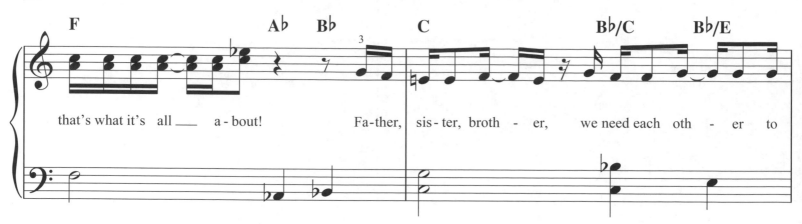

that's what it's all ___ a - bout! Fa - ther, sis - ter, broth - er, we need each oth - er to

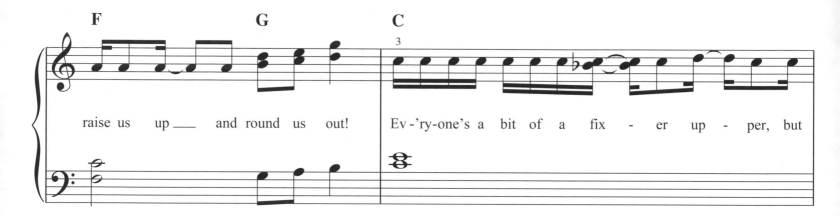

raise us up ___ and round us out! Ev -'ry-one's a bit of a fix - er up - per, but

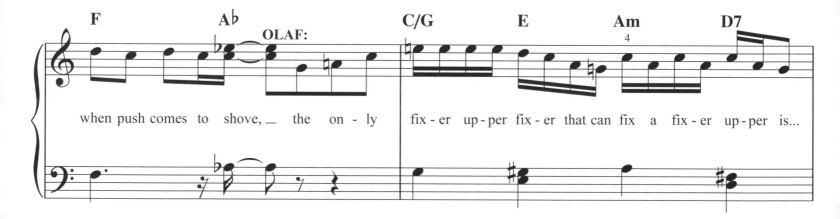

OLAF:
when push comes to shove, __ the on - ly fix - er up - per fix - er that can fix a fix - er up - per is...

MEN & WOMEN:
True, (true,) true, (true,) true, true, true ___

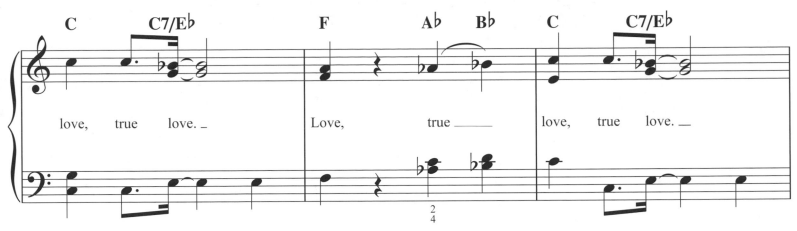

love, true love. ___   Love,   true _____ love, true love. ___

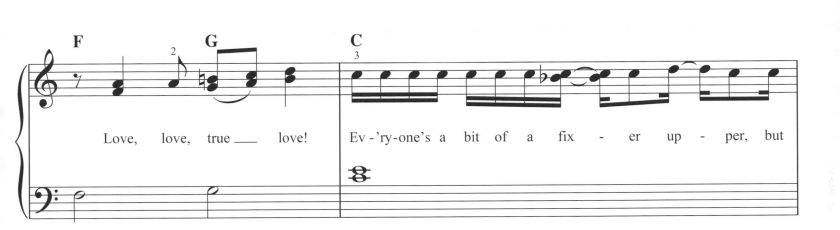

Love, love, true ___ love!   Ev-'ry-one's a bit of a fix - er up - per, but

ver - y wor - thy of ___   love,   love! True   love!

True love!

KRISTOFF LULLABY

Music and Lyrics by KRISTEN ANDERSON-LOPEZ
and ROBERT LOPEZ

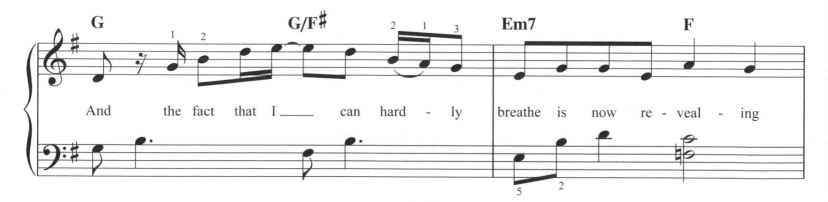

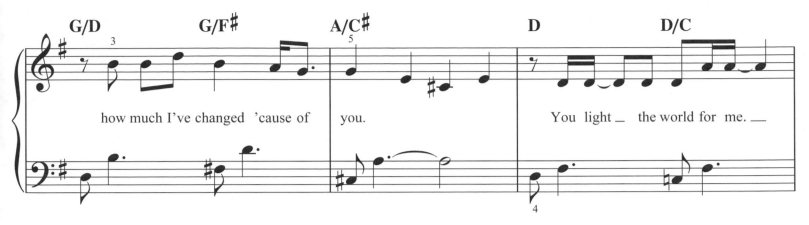

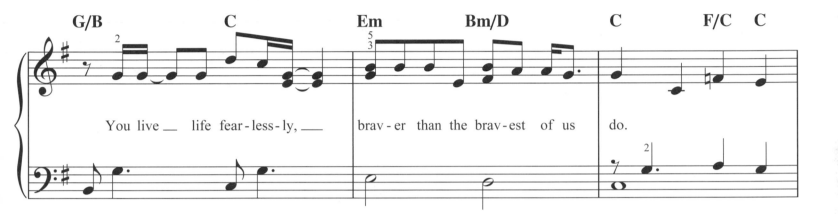

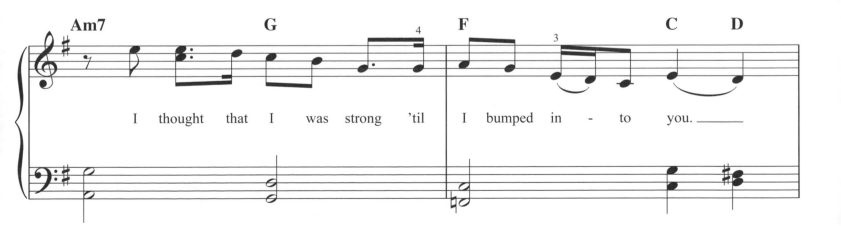

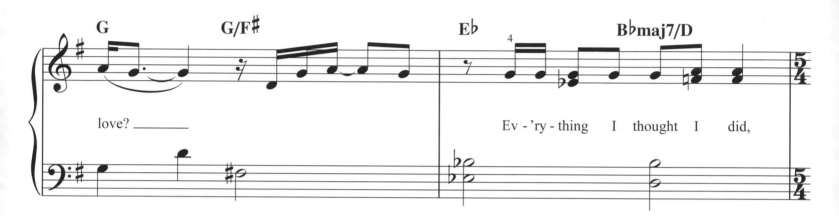

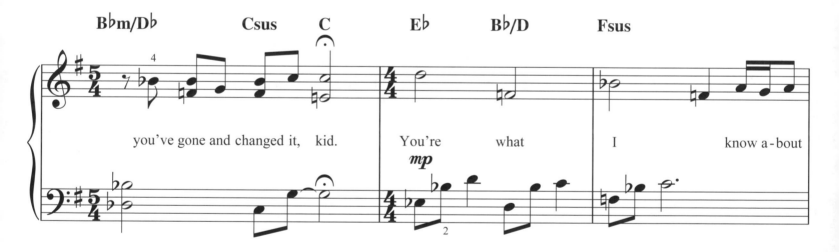

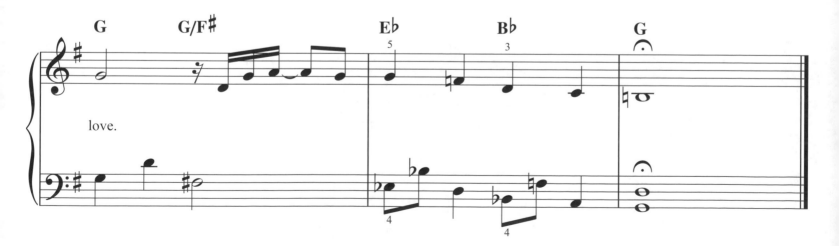

MONSTER

Music and Lyrics by KRISTEN ANDERSON-LOPEZ
and ROBERT LOPEZ

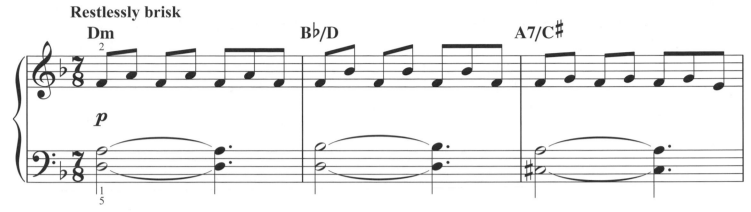

Fear will be your en - e - my and death its con - se - quence. — That's what they once said to me, — and it's

start - ing to make sense. All this pain, all this fear be - gan be - cause of me.

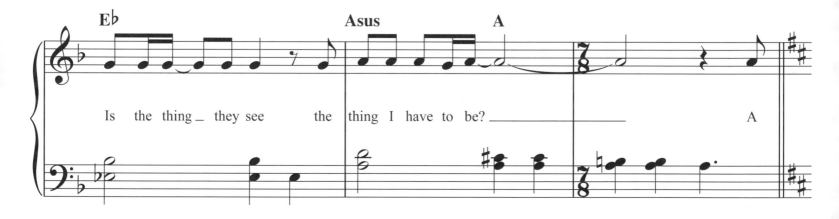

Is the thing — they see the thing I have to be? A

mon - ster. Were they right? Has the dark in me fin - 'lly come to

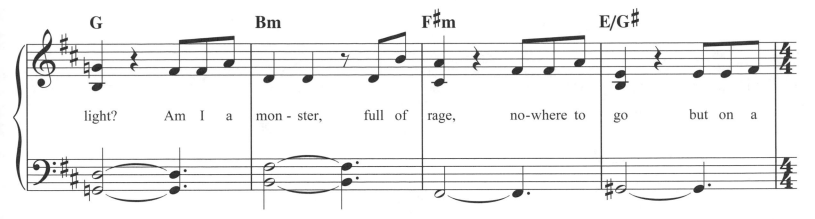

up!

ELSA:
What do I do? No time for cry-ing now. I

start-ed a storm, got-ta stop it some-how. Do I keep on run-ning? How

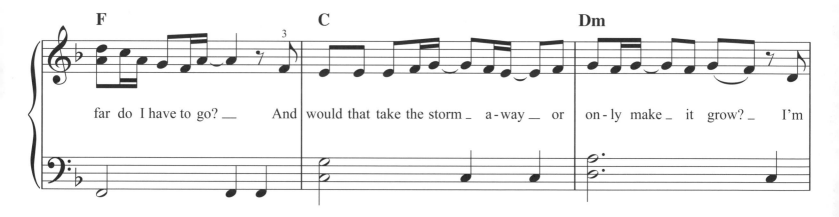

far do I have to go? __ And would that take the storm __ a-way __ or on-ly make __ it grow? __ I'm

mak-ing my world cold-er. How long can it sur-vive? __ Is ev-'ry-one __ in dan-ger as

long as I'm a-live? _ Was I a mon-ster from the start? How did

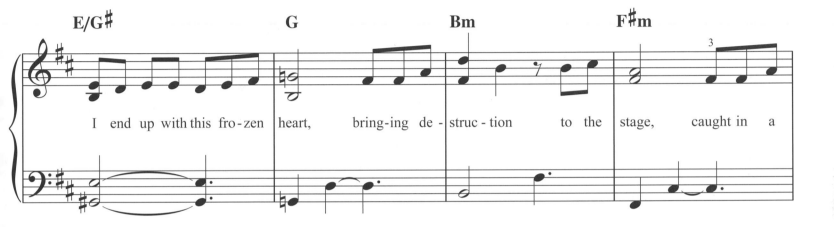

I end up with this fro-zen heart, bring-ing de-struc-tion to the stage, caught in a

war that I nev-er meant to wage? Do I kill the mon - ster?

Fa-ther, you know what's best for me. _ If I die, _ will

they be free?   Moth - er,   what if   af - ter I'm gone   the

cold gets cold - er   and the   storm rag - es on? ___   No!   I have to stay a - live ___ to

fix what I've done. _   Save the world ___   from my - self   and   bring   back ___ the

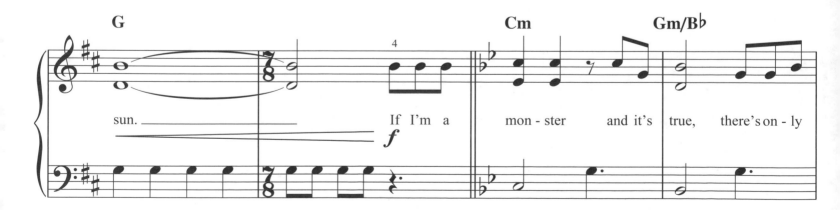

sun. _____   If I'm a   mon - ster   and it's   true,   there's on - ly

one thing that's left for me to do. But be - fore I fade to white, _ I'll do

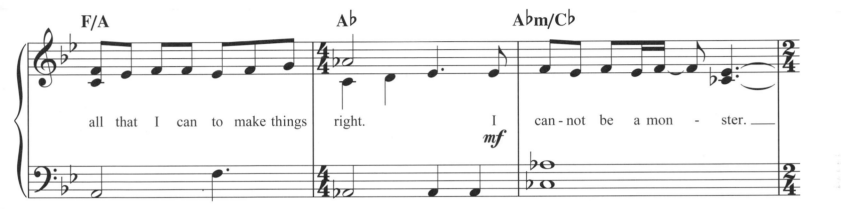

all that I can to make things right. I can - not be a mon - ster. ___

___ I will not be a mon - ster. ___ Not to - night! _

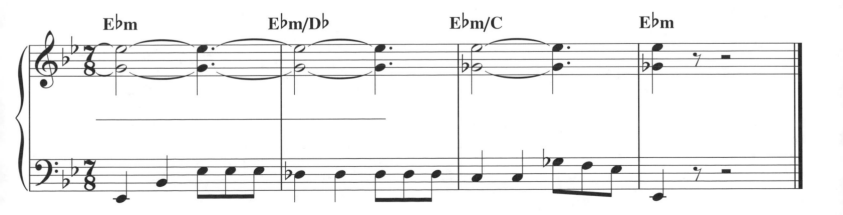

TRUE LOVE

Music and Lyrics by KRISTEN ANDERSON-LOPEZ
and ROBERT LOPEZ

I've sat a - lone in this room _____ be - fore, _____
And here I am in this room _____ a - gain,

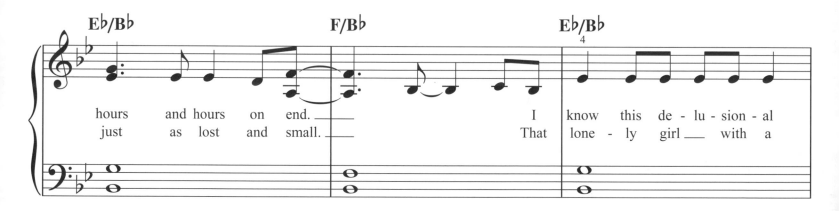

hours and hours on end. _____
just as lost and small. _____

I know this de - lu - sion - al
That lone - ly girl _____ with a

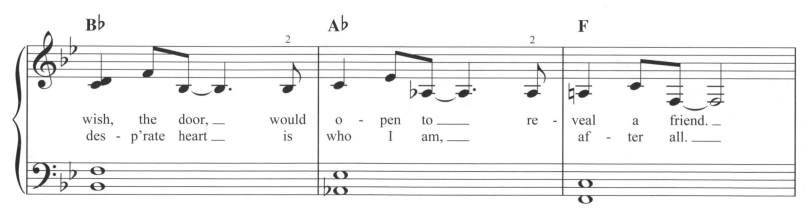

wish, the door, _____ would o - pen to _____ re - veal a friend. _____
des - p'rate heart _____ is who I am, _____ af - ter all. _____

Bb

I know this sol - i - tude,
There's no es - cap - ing her,

F/Bb

I know this kind of cold,
but now the dream is gone

Eb/Bb

but I had faith in what the
be - cause I spent a life - time

1.

Dm

sto - ries told ___ of true ___ love. ___

How I'd find

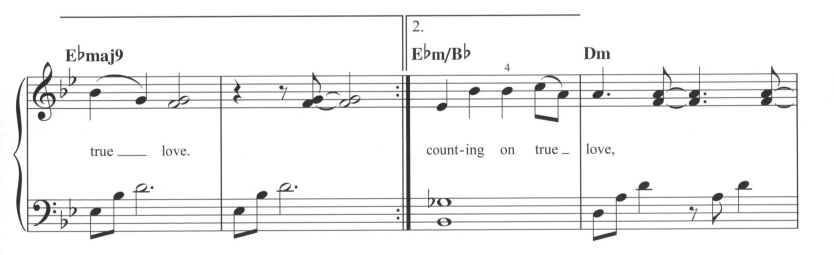

Ebmaj9

true ___ love.

2.

Ebm/Bb

Dm

count - ing on true _ love,

Ebmaj9

true ___ love. ___

I was look-ing for a fair-y tale and dove head-first in-to his.

Turns out, you can't find love if you don't know what it is.

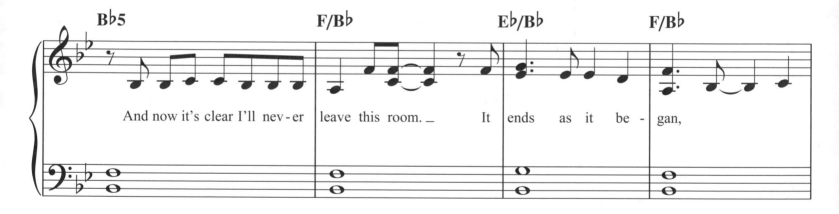

And now it's clear I'll nev-er leave this room. __ It ends as it be-gan,

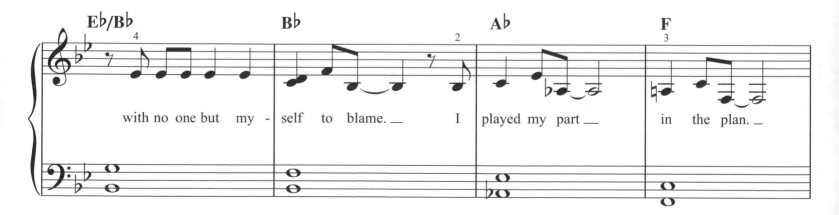

with no one but my-self to blame. __ I played my part __ in the plan. __

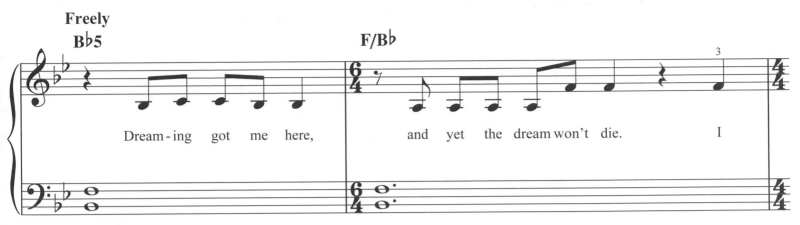

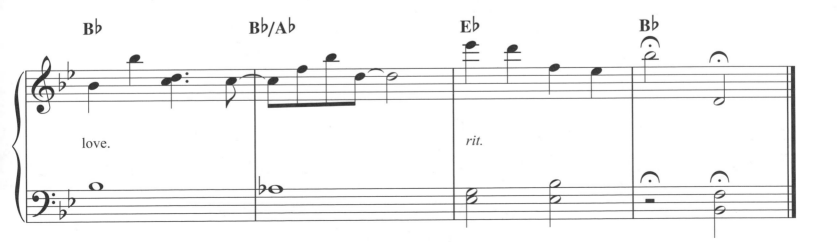

COLDER BY THE MINUTE

Music and Lyrics by KRISTEN ANDERSON-LOPEZ
and ROBERT LOPEZ

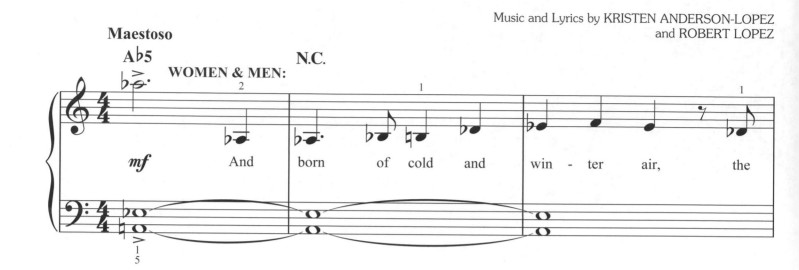

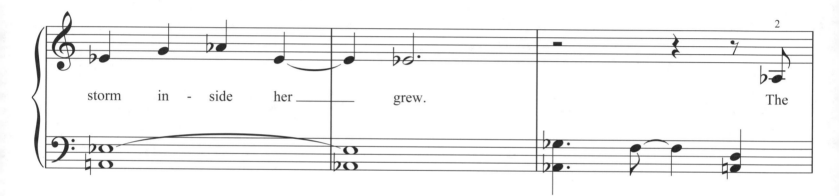

HANS: *I charge Queen Elsa of Arendelle with treason and sentence her to death.*

Ah _____ oh. Ah _____ oh. Ah _____ oh.

Faster

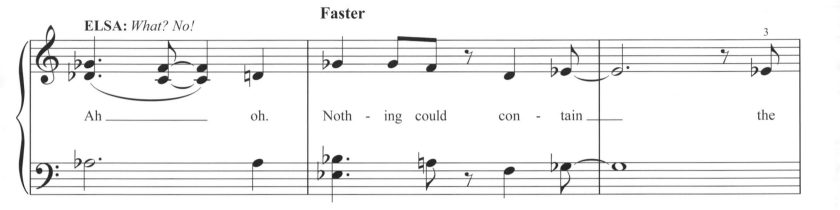

ELSA: *What? No!*

Ah _____ oh. Noth - ing could con - tain _____ the

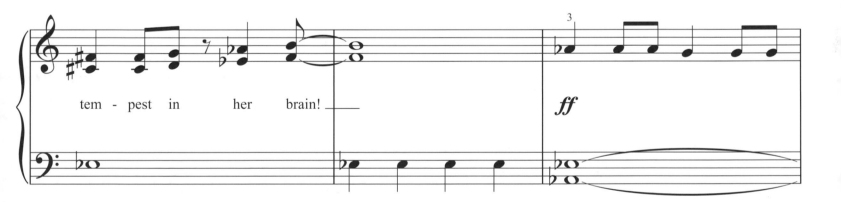

tem - pest in her brain! _____

ff

And the

storm raged __ on, _____ and they were rav - aged by __ the wrath __

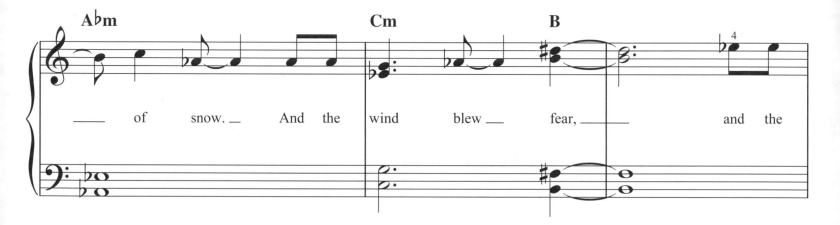

__ of snow. __ And the wind blew __ fear, _____ and the

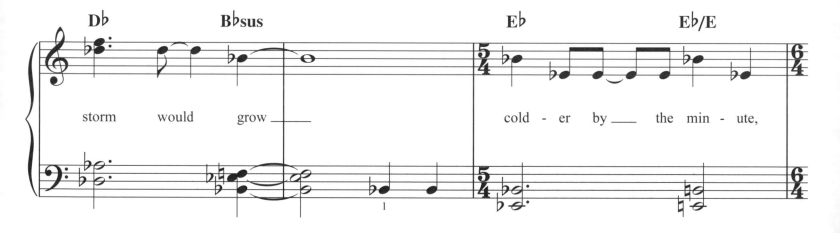

storm would grow _____ cold - er by __ the min - ute,

cold - er by __ the min - ute. Keep walk-ing, An - na, don't stop, don't rest. __

He's out here some-where. ____

I can feel the ice

in my chest, __

in my heart, __

I don't care. __

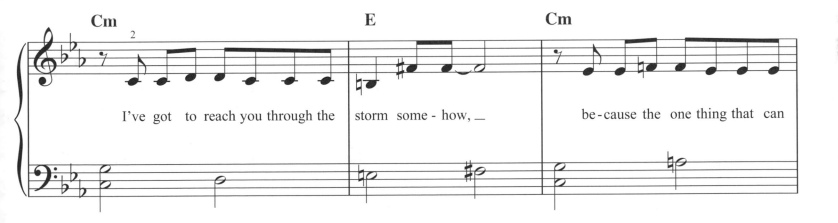

I've got to reach you through the

storm some-how, __

be-cause the one thing that can

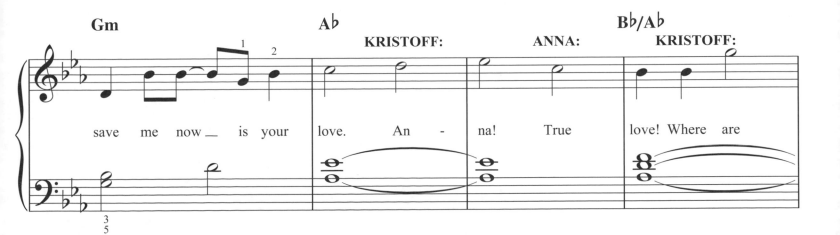

save me now __ is your

KRISTOFF: love. An -

ANNA: na! True

KRISTOFF: love! Where are

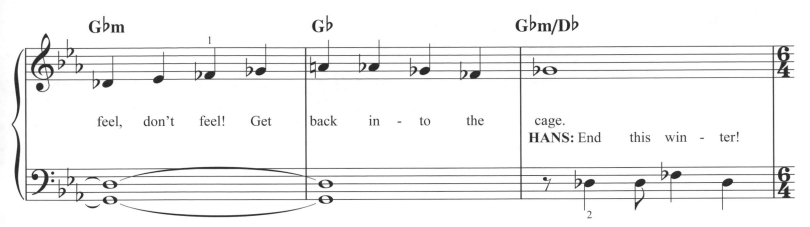

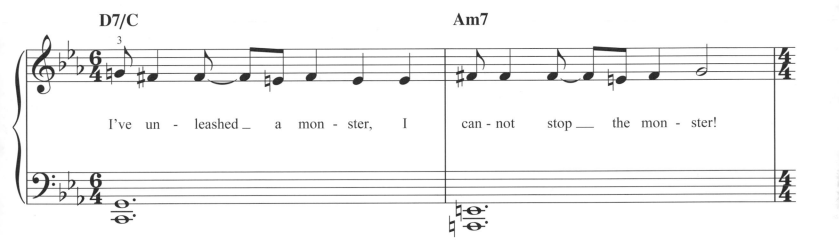

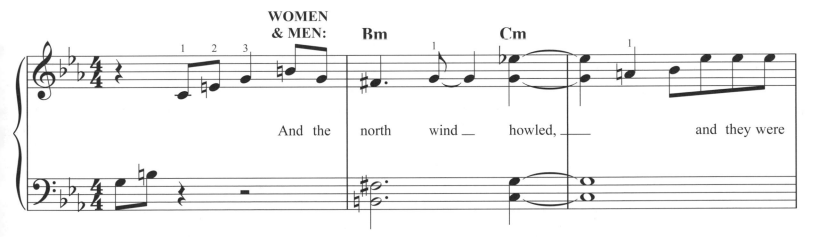

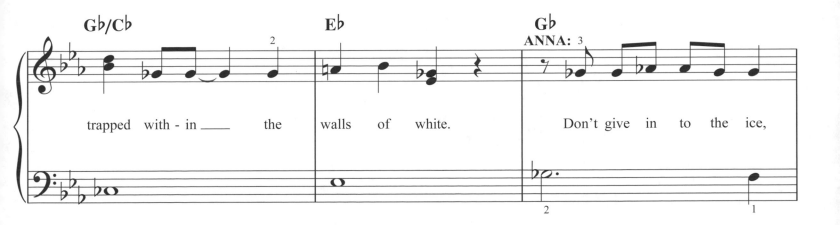

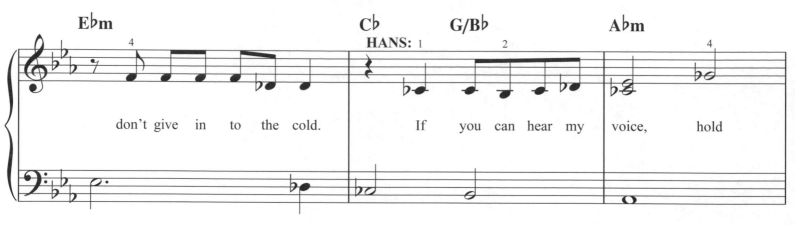

Ebm
don't give in to the cold.
Cb   G/Bb
HANS:
If you can hear my voice, hold
Abm

Bbm
on,   An - na.
ELSA:
I
Ebm
HANS:
can't! El - sa!
WOMEN & MEN:
And the

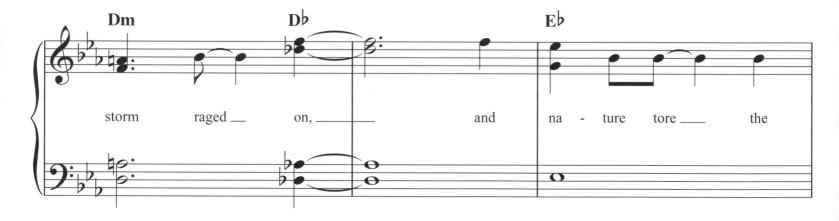

Dm
storm raged __ on, __
Db
and
Eb
na - ture tore __ the

world a - part. And
Dm
all was __ lost __
Db
to the

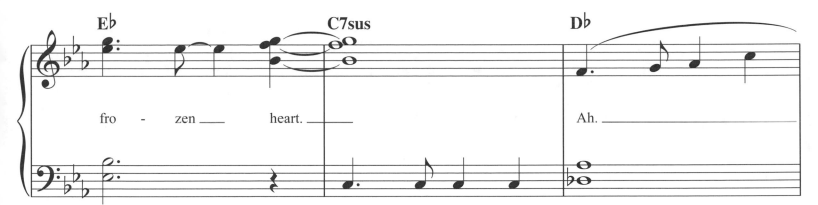

fro - zen ___ heart. ___

Ah. ___

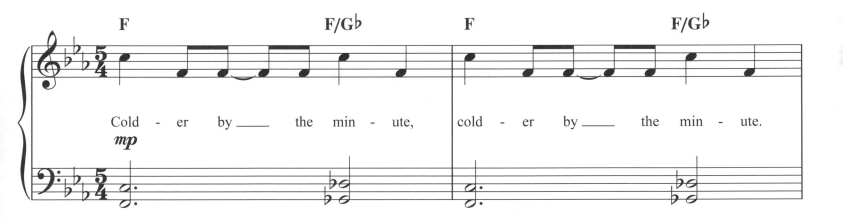

Ah. ___

Cold - er by ___ the min - ute,   cold - er by ___ the min - ute.

mp

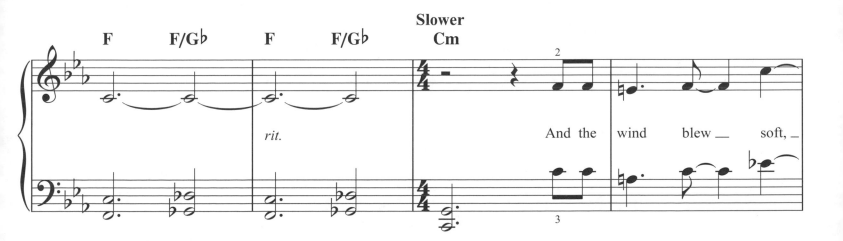

rit.

And the   wind   blew ___ soft, ___

and in her grief, the storm stood — still.

mf

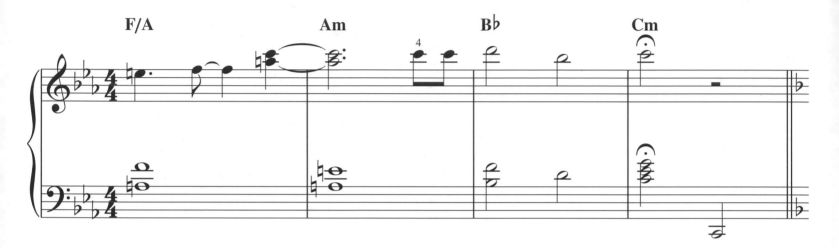

F/A Am B♭ Cm

Moderately fast

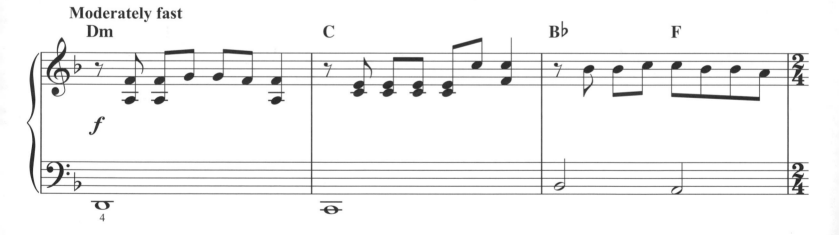

Dm C B♭ F

f

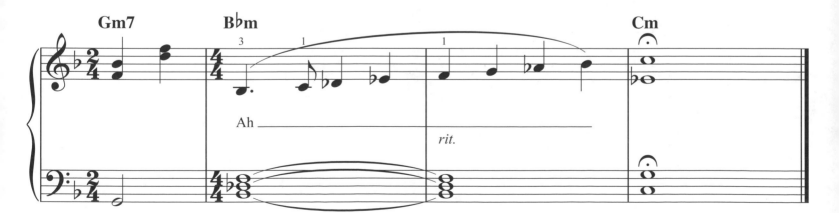

Gm7 B♭m Cm

Ah _____

rit.